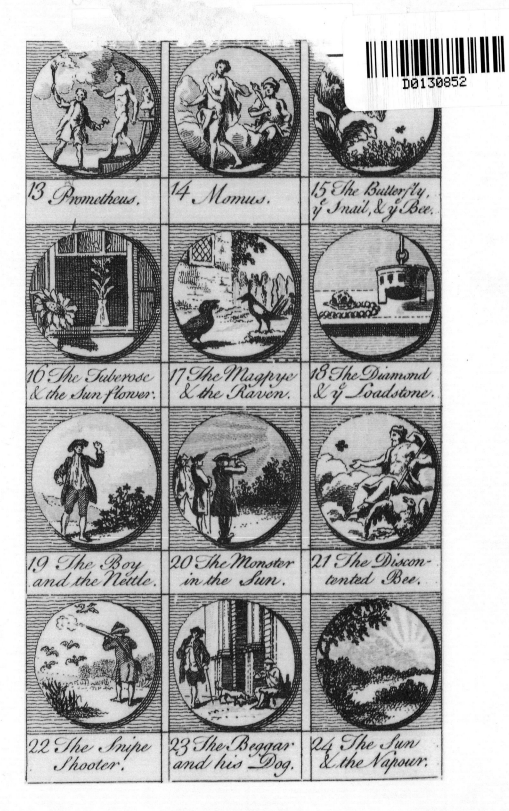

13 Prometheus.

14 Momus.

15 The Butterfly, ye Snail, & ye Bee.

16 The Tuberose & the Sun flower.

17 The Magpye & the Raven.

18 The Diamond & ye Loadstone.

19 The Boy and the Nettle.

20 The Monster in the Sun.

21 The Discontented Bee.

22 The Snipe Shooter.

23 The Beggar and his Dog.

24 The Sun & the Vapour.

FABLES

FABLES

EDITED BY
ANNE STEVENSON HOBBS

VICTORIA AND ALBERT MUSEUM

Published by the Victoria and Albert Museum
First published in 1986

©Trustees of the Victoria and Albert Museum

ISBN 0 948107 12 X

Designed and produced by Patrick Yapp
Printed in Great Britain by
Butler & Tanner Ltd, Frome and London

ENDPAPERS: Four plates from *Select Fables of Esop and Other Fabulists*, collected and edited by Robert Dodsley and printed by John Baskerville of Birmingham for Robert & James Dodsley in London, 1761 (8vo.) 221-1889
   The eminent printer Baskerville departs from routine fable-book layout: normally one plate to every opening. Instead, twelve designs are crowded together in tabular form – in spite of accomplished vignette headpieces by Grignion after Wale, the illustrations were intended to take second place. Richardson did likewise in his 1740 *Aesop*, but he hoped to attract children, to 'excite their curiosity, & stimulate their attention' by including ten fables on each plate. Here, each picture is only one inch square yet contains all the essential elements skilfully dovetailed.

REVERSE OF FRONTISPIECE: 'The Rival Fishes' (detail) from the *Dialogus creaturarum*, 1509   12.viii.1865

TITLE PAGE: Aesop surrounded by symbols of his fables, from *Buch und Leben des hochberühmten Fabeldichters Aesopi*, a facsimile of Heinrich Steinhöwel's German edition (printed in 1476/77 by Zainer of Ulm), edited by Richard Benz and published by Piper of Munich, 1925   L.1029-1947
   The twenty-four symbols, read from right to left, are reminders of incidents in Aesop's career and also of contemporary Renaissance interest in emblems and hieroglyphs: they follow the hieroglyphic pattern of a twenty-four-letter alphabet. Steinhöwel (pp. 13, 15, 34) had been responsible for the introduction of Humanist materials to Germany, but the inaccurate copying of the same symbols for Caxton's English *Aesop* indicates a growing incomprehension of the original meanings.

Contents

... there's a Great Difference, betwixt carrying the *Image* to the *Man*, and bringing the *Man* to the *Image*; Or, ... betwixt Pointing at the *Vice*, or at the *Person*.

L'Estrange: *To the Reader*, 1699

List of Colour Illustrations

Acknowledgements

This book is dedicated to the late Gerald McPherson of the National Art Library, in affectionate memory of his inspiration and support, and to the late Edward Hodnett, who fuelled my enthusiasm and lent me his manuscript concordance of Aesop illustrations.

I am greatly indebted to the designer Patrick Yapp, the photographers Richard Davis and Philip de Bay, the typist Barbara Cole, and the Fish Section of the Department of Zoology, Natural History Museum.

I should also like to thank the following for help, encouragement and advice: my aunt Elisabeth Adams, Julia Bigham, the Rev D. C. Carter, Philippa Glanville, Michael Glover, Judith Haworth, Dr Mary Hobbs, Carol Hogben, Lida Klausner, R.W. Lightbown, Iona Opie, Dr Dolf Polak, Virginia Renshaw, Andrew Topsfield, John and Kate Veale, Caroline Wakely, Dr Rowan Watson, Michael Wilson, James Yorke, and above all my mother and brother for endurance, forbearance and comments on style.

I am grateful to the following for permission to reproduce texts, types and/or illustrations (in order of appearance): *Buch und Leben des hochberühmten Fabeldichters Aesopi* (© R. Piper & Co Verlag, München 1925); Caxton's *Esope* (Gregynog Press); Alfred Caldecott (Macmillan & Co); V.S. Vernon Jones (William Heinemann), Arthur Rackham (Mrs Barbara Edwards); André Hellé (Berger-Levrault); David Jones, Victor Scholderer (The Monotype Corporation PLC), W. H. Shewring (W. H. Shewring); Agnes Miller Parker (Gregynog Press); Willi Harwerth, Rudolf Koch (D. Stempel AG); Stephen Gooden, Sir Edward Marsh (William Heinemann); Marc Chagall (A.D.A.G.P.); Antonio Frasconi (© DACS), Glenway Wescott (The Museum of Modern Art, New York © renewed 1982); Abram Krol, André Moret (Abram Krol); Alexander Calder (A.D.A.G.P.); Felix Hoffmann (Frau Gretel Hoffmann), Victor Zobel (Angelus Druck); and to quote extensively from works by Edward Hodnett (Scolar Press and University of Virginia Bibliographical Society).

Apologia

This book attempts to show a cross-section of fable illustration in printed books from the collections of the National Art Library. The selection necessarily represents only part of the Library's holdings of fable-books and inevitably some distinguished editions are omitted, their artists and authors mentioned only in passing. The arrangement is chronological, the interdependence of editions and interweaving of influences making impracticable any further subdivision. In the interests of digestibility, some dates and all detailed references have been banished to the Index and the Bibliography; for the same reasons bibliographical descriptions are brief.

Included are the *Naples Aesop* of 1485, sixteenth- and seventeenth-century editions with designs by Gheeraerts, Hollar and Barlow, Oudry's *La Fontaine* of 1755–59, the wood engravings of Bewick and Tenniel, the *Gregynog Aesop* of 1931 with woodcuts by Agnes Miller Parker, and the matchless 'livre d'artiste' *La Fontaine* of Chagall.

The fable-text has wherever possible been taken from the book illustrated on the facing page, in which case no attribution is given, or from an edition nearly contemporary with the illustration. Where no appropriate equivalent exists in the Library collections, the editor – without attempting to convert La Fontaine into English verse – provides a translation of the original. In recent years there has been renewed interest in earlier versions, a tendency here reflected in the choice of text. Across a wide spectrum of styles, poetry in varying metre contrasts with prose. An unusual feature is the analysis of fables according to their morals.

Stories both familiar and unfamiliar are recorded in this anthology from a particularly beguiling form of picture book.

> An ample Comedy of a hundred acts diverse,
> Whose setting is the Universe.
>
> La Fontaine: Book V, i

RANA RUPTA ET BOS.
FAB. XXIV.

CANIS ET CROCODILUS.
FAB. XXV.

VULPIS ET CICONIA.
FAB. XXVI.

CANIS ET THESAURUS ET VULTURIUS.
FAB. XXVII.

VULPIS ET AQUILA.
FAB. XXVIII.

ASINUS IRRIDENS APRUM.
FAB. XXIX.

A. v. d. Aa fecit et del.

5

Five Hundred Years of Illustration and Text

Fables were the first pieces of wit that made their appearance in the world, and have been still highly valued not only in times of the greatest simplicity, but among the most polite ages of mankind.

Addison: *Spectator* 183, 29 Sept 1711

A fable is a short dramatic tale with an unmistakeable 'moral' and a cast of animals or inanimate objects representing stock human characters. Fable-actors must be 'like abstractions in algebra, or like pieces in chess' (Chesterton 1912): creatures become heraldic symbols and human beings with their complex psychology are banished to the background.

The Orientalist Sir Richard Burton judged that 'man's use of the beast-fable commemorates our instinctive knowledge of how we emerged from the animal kingdom' or from an epoch when man lived in closer contact with animals. It was natural for primitive man to invent stories about beasts and to draw them on the walls of caves. The fable or folk tale with a wily animal hero coexists with anthropomorphic myths: beasts behave according to received ideas about their natures based on observation or legend. The symbolic qualities of animals have ancient roots: even the fox of Babylonia was already a cunning deceiver, and by the time that animals were clothed and thoroughly humanised the stereotypes had become fixed. Behaviour and events are unlikely but 'inside the circle of possible things' (E. Nesbit: *The Enchanted Castle*), and even the bizarre seems acceptable.

Fables combine admonition with amusement and often satire; they gently cajole the recipient into understanding – they are puzzles concealing hidden truths. 'Aesop's' language was spare and pithy, his message unstated. Gradually explicit morals became attached, originating in the Indian *Jātakas*. The moral came to be regarded as an essential element, even preceding and dominating the story, and acquiring a 'load of accumulated reflections' (Dodsley). Dodsley criticised the use of high-flown artificial language, pointing out that an unaffected style is the hardest to achieve. He urged fable-writers to adapt their idiom to occasion and personality.

Like the anecdote – the briefest and probably the earliest fictional form – a fable describes a single event with a beginning, middle and end, and some sort of punch line. Fables, like folk tales, are short and plain, tending to concentrate on black and white at the expense of grey – but fables have an altogether sterner purpose. A folk tale may have the consolation of a happy ending, but a fable has a sting in

OPPOSITE: Plate from David Hoogstraten's edition of Phaedrus, printed by Franciscus Halma of Amsterdam, 1701 (4to.)   25.iii.1865

A fable edition prepared for the young Prince of Nassau, whose portrait precedes the fables (see p. 31). Large clear print makes the fable-texts more inviting, as do Jan van Vianen's vivacious engravings in a series of medallions, many depicting scenes from Dutch life of the period (in the 1704 edition they appear as separate plates). The composition is divided into several layers: a customary method of simultaneously presenting each episode, as if a frieze in depth.

its tail or at least ends on a resigned or pessimistic note. Fables share none of the heroism, illusion and wonder of fairy tale and legend; there is no place for wishful thinking in their cosmography. (Origin myths again are primitive and timeless, but seek to explain the universe rather than comment on the world of man.)

Closer to Aesop is the wisdom-literature of Egypt, and parables, both Christian and Indian (see also p. 40); related too are *exempla*, moral stories adopted by preachers and teachers in the Middle Ages. Not to be confused with fables are *fabliaux*, short comic verse tales of everyday life. The adjective 'fabulous' is less specific: it refers to the legendary, fictitious or absurd. Bestiaries were mediaeval treatises deriving from the Greek *Physiologus*, a collection of 'fabulous' anecdotes – and some 'fabulous beasts' – from natural history (see Darton, p. 28). Both bestiaries and *Physiologus* describe traditional animal characteristics; every creature stands for a human virtue or vice (see also pp. 40, 132, 134). Each genre was not only a source of fresh fable material but depended on fables for its own survival.

Fables are distinguished from other animal stories and from parables by the substitution of animals for humans, as in *Reynard the Fox*, a box-within-a-box narrative structure otherwise unknown in the West. The satirical beast epic is a form now dead in which animals act out the human drama, parodying the romances of chivalry. The *Reynard* tales, mainly of Eastern origin but infiltrated by mediaeval Latin poems, were known in North-West Europe before Aesop; they too contained episodes based on fables. Both bestiary and fabulists' fox are drawn into the *Roman de Renard* (c. 1175). The earliest printed *Reynard the Fox* (Leeu of Gouda, 1479) was followed by Caxton's unillustrated and now rare edition of 1481. As a favourite of the Norman court *Reynard* was not widely read in England nor much used by preachers, though Ogilby and L'Estrange attempted to re-create the form. Intended for the general reader but often revived for children, it was never so highly regarded here as on the Continent. The Fox (unnamed in Greek fables) was always prominent in Western folk tale, pitted against Wolf or Bear. In the thirteenth century it replaced the wolf Ysengrim as arch-hypocrite; in the transfer of folklore from East to West it ousts the Oriental jackal.

Aesop's common sense and wisdom is based on observation of human behaviour. He recommends the peasant virtues of 'discretion, prudence, moderation and foresight' (Reeves), which sometimes prevail over orthodox morality. The Persians praised *Kalīlah wa-Dimnah* (p. 41) as 'a book which the wise love for its wisdom and the foolish for its entertainment'. The lowest and highest can learn from fables (Luther 1530); they can help 'al maner of folk' (Caxton). Their unadorned brevity and wit make them approachable by the simplest minds; their neatness and inevitability give a profounder pleasure to the more sophisticated. Often quoted in theological argument, political debate and literary satire, fables offered a safe weapon against established authority (see p. 31) under despotic governments where open opposition was impossible. Fables teach home truths without causing offence or hurting the pride: most people dislike having their faults exposed but are willing to listen to criticism once removed, told in a fable to someone else and an animal at that (Luther). If one's wits are set to guessing the moral, one's self-esteem remains unscathed. The lesson is most effective if implicit: a moral at the start spoils one's pleasure, as acknowledged by La Motte – who stressed that reflection and story should be inseparable, but headed his own fables with wordy prologues! The more entertaining a fable, the more impression it makes: 'badiner pour instruire'.

Fables, part of formal education from ancient times, taught rhetoric and morality to the young and instilled, directly and by allusion, sound principles of statecraft in future rulers. The educational value of fables lies in their subconscious appeal, free from the religious or mythological connotations of more obviously edifying texts. Their charm lies in the superficial clarity which conceals their complexity.

History of the Texts

Grand rough old Martin Luther
  Bloomed fables – flowers on furze,
The better the uncouther:
  Do roses stick like burrs?

Robert Browning: *The Twins*

Fables originated in Greece, probably in Asia Minor. They appear in poetry of the eighth century BC, long before the earliest known fables of any other country. Hesiod and Archilochus quote fables but Homer contains none. Aristophanes, Plato and Aristotle refer to fables; Socrates translated them in prison. The first collection and still the most famous is associated with the name of Aesop, an obscure, semi-legendary figure whom Herodotus called 'maker of stories'. Aesop was apparently a deformed and illiterate Thracian slave who lived on Samos with his masters, first Xanthos and then Iadmon, in the sixth century BC. He travelled widely, and became favourite and ambassador of Croesus. Arbitrating in disputes by telling pointed fables, he won fame and eventually freedom through his skill, though often at loggerheads with the established priesthood. The people of Delphi accused him of sacrilege and hurled him from a precipice; calamities beset them till reparation had been made – hence the saying 'the blood of Aesop' (murder will be avenged). Immortalised in a statue by Lysippus and a portrait by Velazquez, and credited with the authorship of all animal fables, Aesop's name became a focus for legend.

Aesop's *Life*, the earliest European 'novel', descends from ancient times; the best-known version (*c.* 1300), by the Byzantine scholar and monk Maximus Planudes, presents him as a grotesque but cheerful scapegoat. On the *Ulm Aesop's* title page (pp. 3–4) Aesop is a crippled, smock-clad slave – mouthpiece of the under-privileged and adviser of kings – revealed as wise instructor by his symbolic ad-monitory gesture. The mediaeval conception of Aesop had been an amiable or idealised one, but the discovery of his *Life* (translated only in 1448 by Rinuccio of Arezzo and first put into German by Steinhöwel) revived ancient traditions with a change in iconography. Illustrations of the *Life* soon became rare except in chap-books; the fables themselves played only a minor part among the ribaldries of the *Life*. Once the subject of a Greek drama, Aesop re-emerged in early eighteenth-century comedy and farce, at a period which briefly restored a more genial figure (see p. 27). L'Estrange reminded his readers that Aesop's message should concern us more than whether he was 'strait or crooked'; Dodsley dwells on his wit and good nature.

Both Aesop and Bīdpāī, his Indian counterpart (pp. 18, 41), have inspired a succession of retellings and translations. There has never been one classic text, so inevitably style has changed according to fashion and individual fancy. The first known written version (now lost) is the fourth-century *Aesopia* of the politician De-metrius of Phalerum – perhaps intended to provide fables as illustrations for other orators. Two later Greek versions survive: the anonymous prose *Augustana* and the verses of Babrius, a Hellenised Roman – discovered only in 1843 on Mount Athos but known in the Middle Ages through an imitation. Greek fables, familiar in ancient Rome, are told by Plutarch and Lucian. The first, most succinct and most polished version combined topical anecdotes with satire: eighty fables in iambics by Phaedrus, a freed slave. A best-seller in his time though ignored by serious critics (times have not changed), he came under suspicion in spite of his discretion. Avianus' fables (*c.* 400 AD), stylistically inferior to Phaedrus, derive mainly from Babrius.

All French and English collections up to the seventeenth century descend from Greek sources: 'our Aesop is Phaedrus with Trimmings' (Jacobs 1889). Phaedrus like Babrius survived in the late Latin prose of 'Romulus', the most widespread fable-book of the Middle Ages – which with Avianus formed a bridge between ancient and mediaeval traditions. The self-styled 'Romulus' collected animal fables, whereas the Greeks included men and gods. Phaedrus (via Romulus) reappears in mediaeval Latin elegiacs as the '*Aesopus moralisatus*', ascribed to Salone of Parma – or more often to the Anonymus Neveleti, alias Walter of England, Bishop of Palermo and Court Chaplain to Henry II. Much translated, it was particularly influential in the *Mythologia Aesopica* of 1610. Each new version was absorbed by the existing fable corpus. 'Aesopic' fables crop up in sermons and school books, political pamphlets and emblem books, clinging together in groups which persist over the centuries. The pagan gods disappear, but return with the Renaissance. Prose and verse have alternated from antiquity till today – but the old tradition of mediaeval rhetoric was long in dying: poetry is falsehood, prose is truth.

Monasteries took a leading part in the dissemination of fables, retrieving ancient materials and adding new discoveries; Fathers of the Church composed fables as did later the Fathers of the Reformation. Both sacred and secular, the Anglo-Norman contribution was considerable. Marie de France quotes a lost book of Alfred the Great as one source of her fables (*c.* 1189) but the only collection in English was made by John Lydgate (*c.* 1390). Another Alfred adapted fables, but into Latin; so too did the grammarian Alexander Neckam in the *Novus Aesopus*. To Alfred de Sareshel, nature was a mirror of human life – as to Vincent de Beauvais (see p. 134), author of the satirical *Speculum doctrinale*. The aristocratic country parson Odo of Cheriton brought original material into his racy Latin verse collection (*c.* 1220), an important source for poets and preachers. Church and Court drew on an already flourishing popular beast-story tradition, and the study of nature was much esteemed. In the rising towns of the late Middle Ages a growing self-awareness expressed itself in every type of animal satire (see p. 12). The motifs, verbal and visual (p. 23), invade every medium; they enrich later versions of *Reynard the Fox*, and *Tyl Eulenspiegel*. Bestiary-writers believed that animals, given symbolic meaning, were created for the edification of mankind. Fable-writers too could not resist the temptation to add a Christian moral and a quotation from the Bible – an adhesive habit which survives in the didactic animal stories of the nineteenth century.

Italy had a much closer association than Northern Europe with Greek traditions, revived through contact with Arab and Jewish scholars. The Humanists translated and so popularised Aesop: this 'new learning', like the Vulgate, reached the vernaculars through Latin versions. Valla and Rinuccio (pp. 13, 39) made the earliest and most widespread translations, but Leonardo da Vinci was the first to compose new fables. The 'first Renaissance *Aesop*', edited by Planudes, was printed by Bonus Accursius (*c.* 1480); for centuries it remained the standard text. The great illustrated translations were by Zucco and del Tuppo – attracting a new public, able to read but only in its own tongue. The printing press made favourite reading matter more accessible, adding the enticement of woodcuts.

The leading fabulist of late mediaeval Central Europe was Ulrich Boner, a monk of Bern who carried on the ancient method of teaching by examples. His couplet verse *Edelstein* (*c.* 1330) popularised the old themes of Avianus and Walter: one of the first collections devoted to fables alone and by a single author, it was also the first printed fable-book. Most popular of all was the *Ulm Aesop* (pp. 3-4, 34), for which Heinrich Steinhöwel collated all the fables known to his period.

In England before 1700 all 'Aesop's Fables' were taken from Steinhöwel. The freest and liveliest early adaptation (apart from Chaucer) was made by the fifteenth-century Scottish poet and pedagogue Robert Henryson: *The Morall Fabillis of Esope the Phrygian* (printed only in 1570). The first published English fable-book was Caxton's *Subtyl Historyes and Fables of Esope* – in print till the 1700s, it became the basis for many children's *Aesops* (see pp. 19, 118). England was now contributing less to the recovery of classical fables and to the writing of new ones. Of the mediaeval Latin collections only Walter's appeared in England. Continental versions were imported, and even the major Greek edition of the seventeenth century, Nevelet's *Mythologia Aesopica* (see above), was published here only after the Restoration. Most Elizabethan authors quote single fables: Donne, Spenser, Jonson's *Volpone*, 'The Belly and the Members' in Shakespeare's *Coriolanus*.

Fables were used in the Reformation as anti-Papist vehicles (p. 31). Luther's version, improving on Steinhöwel, was never independently published. Erasmus of Rotterdam compiled proverbs (1500); Erasmus Alberus, schoolmaster and pastor, blended local colour with strict moral teaching in his fables (1550) which like those of Burkhard Waldis and Hans Sachs are addressed at least partly to the young. Later in the century the centre of gravity shifted to the Netherlands, where fables were partially eclipsed by a new genre: the emblem book. The name was devised by Alciati: 'emblems' were symbolic pictures verbally interpreted (see pp. 26-7, 42-3). Fables cross-fertilised with emblem books, and for many years the two genres coexisted. Fable motifs were kept alive by great preachers such as Abraham à Sancta Clara, and textual continuity ensured not only by classroom use but by the persistence of fables in 'reader-friendly' everyday books. In Germany especially, plainer low-cost editions made *Aesops* available to the man in the street. Aesop – but not La Fontaine – always remained part of folk-literature in crude chapbooks carried far and wide by pedlars.

In France literacy was more general but fables reached fewer people. Fables were still taken for granted as inherited wisdoms; Rabelais' Gargantua quotes them, for instance. In the early seventeenth century rhyme was again condemned, and it was considered a fable's chief ornament to have none – but La Fontaine's subtle masterpieces lifted fables out of the schoolroom, to which they would soon return as classic texts for the young.

La Fontaine created a poetry of fable, causing it to be regarded for the first time as literature; in France he was even compared with Homer and Shakespeare. His 'vers irréguliers', part verse, part prose, employ a variety of rhyme forms and an idiom that moves from the elegant to a more characteristic witty 'genteel familiar' (Dodsley). Master of Waters and Forests like his father and grandfather before him, La Fontaine is remembered today almost entirely for his two hundred and forty fables, and the more risqué *Contes*. In 1684 he was made a member of the French Academy, against the wish of Louis XIV who disliked his liberal views. The fables (printed by Barbin and Thierry) appeared between 1668 and 1694 in twelve books and met instant success; already in 1672 a child in Molière's *Le Malade imaginaire* offers to tell her father 'The Cock and the Fox'. La Fontaine aimed above all to please, and to encourage wisdom and virtue in young and old.

A host of influences lay behind La Fontaine's fables: Aesopic motifs from Phaedrus – he has been called 'mainly Phaedrus transmuted from silver to gold', the *Mythologia Aesopica*, Oriental fables and the *Dialogus creaturarum* (pp. 38-9), and maxims from Plato and Plutarch. He had seen both emblem books and emblematic fables by Baudoin, Perret and Trichet du Fresne (in Sadeler's version) and knew the *Esbatement moral* (pp. 46-7) in its reprint, the *Théâtre des animaux*. Books VII to XI, derived more from Bīdpāī, are political and contemplative – and, unlike the other books, not dedicated to a child. Yet La Fontaine's fables seem fresh, and free from local or contemporary fashion. His international popularity springs from the universality of his appeal. Poets in the wake of La Fontaine competed to emulate him, with varying degrees of success. The second most famous French fabulist was Houdart de La Motte, 'father of fable theory', whose unrealised ambition was to be Aesop and La Fontaine rolled into one. His 'literary' and longwinded fables were intended as a courtesy manual and, incidentally, to please the Court. Archbishop Fénelon composed fables as well as *The Adventures of Telemachus* for the Duke of Burgundy, grandson of Louis XIV – to whose father La Fontaine had dedicated his Books I-VI, and who was himself the recipient of Book XII.

Prosaic in comparison were John Brinsley in Latin, and William Barret, who replaced Caxton as the cheap edition in English. The last version before the Restoration was also the finest: *Fables of Aesop Paraphras'd in Verse* by John Ogilby (pp. 54-9), who set a fashion for fables in England even before La Fontaine had been published in France. Robert Thomson made the first verse translation of La Fontaine – but he originally appeared in English in the 1699 sequel to L'Estrange's *Fables of Aesop, and Other Eminent Mythologists*. Sir Roger L'Estrange, Catholic and Royalist, meant to replace the 'Insipid & Flat' morals with his ribald and controversial collection of five hundred fables, the largest in English. Dodsley exaggerates in condemning L'Estrange as 'coarse and vulgar', but only Caxton is more popular with modern editors.

The worthy and humourless Dr Croxall unjustly accuses L'Estrange of Papist bigotry and slavish doctrines, highly unsuitable for the children of Britain, 'for they are born with free blood in their veins, and suck in liberty with their very milk'. Croxall (pp. 84-6) dedicated his own unobjectionably dull fables of 1722 to the five-year-old paragon, Baron Halifax. Samuel Richardson valued Liberty, and abstracted his fables 'from all party considerations'. His comments on Croxall's horror of L'Estrange make amusing reading: these 'terrible apprehensions ... are merely the effects of the good Doctor's imagination' and Croxall 'little considers ... how liable he himself is to objection, for his pedantick quotation and Latin scraps'. In contrast, Richardson's prose (p. 72) has the elegance of balance and restraint.

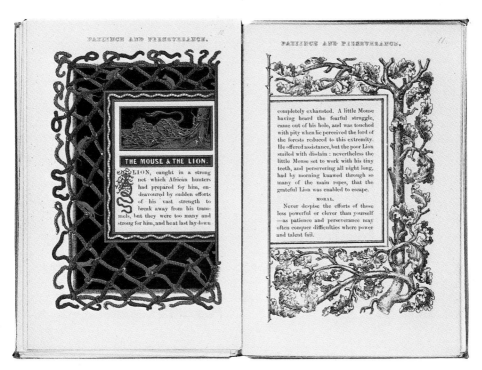

'The Mouse and the Lion',
from *The Child's Illuminated Fable-Book*, 1847 (see pp. 92-3)

Dodsley's celebrated improvement of L'Estrange (pp. 4, 120), complete with an 'Essay on Fable' cribbed from La Motte, included some original fables - but the best-known English fabulist is John Gay (pp. 70-1, 80-1). His fables were cultivated, literary and complex, without the single telling Aesopian maxim. Gay like La Fontaine dedicated his first volume (1727) to a 'young Prince', the six-year-old Duke of Cumberland. He wooed Court recognition, and his subject-matter is often relevant to Court life, but the sixteen meatier two-part fables of his second collection are less well-disposed towards authority and not deliberately educational. Gay's fables were issued repeatedly in fine editions and remained in print well into the next century. Children read them chiefly in anthologies, but 'Hare and Many Friends' often appeared separately and with a more bloodthirsty dénouement.

The new wave of 'literary' fables had come from France, and La Fontaine was much admired by the arrogant Age of Reason. Between 1740 and 1770 there was a positive epidemic of fables in Germany, where famous poets exploited the form, believing it their task to uncover the truth. Goethe valued fables for their imitation of nature and moral usefulness. The incisive prose of Lessing - progressive social critic, leading theoretician of fable and a despiser of ornament - sharply contrasts with the less demanding verse *divertissements* of Gellert and later, kindlier narrations by the German or Swiss Romantics: Herder, Fröhlich (illustrated by Disteli), the reformer Pestalozzi. The most distinguished fable-poet of the nineteenth century was Kruilov, the 'Russian La Fontaine': the only East European fabulist of any real repute. More vehement than his namesake and inveighing against hypocrisy, Kruilov is hardly read in the West - but Russian children, Chagall included, knew him as well as French children knew their La Fontaine.

With the increasing dominance of juvenile versions (p. 22), fables recovered a moral and even a Christian purpose. Illustration takes precedence over text, now often insipid. Selections for the young usually keep to simple tales with an obvious story-line, so preserving the authentic Aesop. Though fables continue to bear visual fruit, as literature for adults they have outlived their vigour. There are some notable exceptions. The folklorist Joseph Jacobs published the first scholarly studies in English: Bīdpāī in 1888, Caxton's *Aesop* in 1889 (and a selection in 1894), *Reynard the Fox* in 1895. Beatrix Potter produced some refreshingly inventive versions: the unpublished 'Sour Grapes' (with its punch line 'That is *not* a fat pigeon'!) and the better-known *Tale of Johnny Town-Mouse*, with its warning about the danger and extravagance of town life. She knew the stories of 'Uncle Remus', a slave like Aesop, whose African stories in an American setting include familiar fables. The provocative journalist Ambrose Bierce (the 'American Swift') and James Thurber (*Fables For Our Time*) echo the black humour and disillusion of Wilhelm Busch's 1870s verse. Since 1945 the impulse to write original fables has taken hold once more, resulting in a number of satirical pieces (p. 31). Classical fable-texts too have been revived: Caxton, L'Estrange, La Fontaine – and in 1982, after several centuries of neglect, Bīdpāī's fables appeared in a new English version.

Bīdpāī, apparently one of only two books to survive the burning of the Library at Alexandria, is hardly known in the West today. The Indian collections, formerly supposed the model for Greek fables, contain nothing earlier than the fourth century BC, but their forebears may rival Aesop in antiquity. The Indians too love stories of animal kinship with a moralising bent, but the two groups are not directly linked (though Aesop has traces of Eastern influence: apes and camels, the 'Man and Two Wives'). The tales of Bīdpāī descend from the *Panchatantra*, the *Hitopadeśa* and the older Buddhist *Jātakas* in two branches, Arabic and Persian. The Arabic branch comes down from the *Kalīlah wa-Dimnah* via the *Directorium humanae vitae* and *Buch der Beispiele der Alten Weisen* (see pp. 40-1) to the first English edition, North's *Morall Philosophie of Doni* (1570). The Old Persian collection, *Anvār-i-Suhailī* or *Lights of Canopus*, again deriving from the Arabic, arrived here later by way of the French *Fables de Pilpay*. Bīdpāī's fables were included in printed *Aesops*, especially for the young – with whom they had less success than Aesop, perhaps because the animals behave too much like humans (Topsfield). Boccaccio and Chaucer drew on Eastern fables as did Shakespeare, who encountered them in the *Gesta Romanorum*, a mediaeval collection of *exempla* which includes the Llewellyn and Gelert legend. Bīdpāī's jackal sneaks back as Reynard the Fox (p. 12).

Fable-beasts have left their mark in folklore and literature of most cultures. Fable-books were among the first to be printed, and only the Bible has travelled farther. No book has been more often illustrated or more read by children.

Fables and Children

Children are but *Blank Paper*, ... and it is much in the Power of the first Comer, to Write Saint, or Devil upon't, which of the Two he pleases. ...

This *Rhapsody* of *Fables* is a Book universally Read, and Taught in all our Schools; but almost at such a Rate as we teach *Pyes* and *Parrots*. ... The Boys break their Teeth upon the Shells, without ever coming near the Kernel. They learn *Fables* by *Lessons*, and the Moral is the least part of our Care in a Child's Institution.

L'Estrange: *Preface*, 1692

Fables were always the inheritance of the illiterate. In the Middle Ages they were addressed primarily to 'Jüngere': those of lowly social standing or tender years. Writers often hesitated to demean themselves by publishing fables: even Ogilby reminds us that no loss of dignity is involved since Socrates himself put Aesop into verse.

Aesop's stories are vivid and energetic, straightforward and full of practical wisdom. It was fondly hoped that his fables would distract children from harmful reading: fairy tales were more often than not frowned upon by the moralists. Even the late seventeenth-century 'conte de fées' flowered in salon rather than nursery. John Locke (*Some Thoughts Concerning Education*, 1693) condemned fairy stories as 'perfectly useless trumpery'; only Aesop and Reynard the Fox served his purpose. The Earl of Chesterfield in a letter to his godson (1764) praised La Fontaine as far more beneficial and diverting than Perrault's frivolous tales of Mother Goose. Fables evolved only gradually as children's literature, by two routes: school or other didactic editions (occasionally with the lure of pictures) and 'polite' editions.

For twenty-five centuries fables helped in the teaching of grammar and syntax and, gradually, in providing moral education unawares. Aesop became part of the curriculum in ancient schools of rhetoric, and the composition of fables in Latin verse was a regular practice in mediaeval and Renaissance Europe. This tradition, not confined to the classroom, was kept alive by preachers and scholars. The Humanists adopted Dorp's *Phaedrus* as the basis for numerous textbook *Aesops* commissioned by the Dutch government, some even illustrated (pp. 52-3). School editions rarely had the luxury of pictures except in Italy or, occasionally, England – and apart from the de Tournes *Aesops* (pp. 42-3). Any ambivalence or unsuitability in the morals may have been avoided by making selections, but the huge Dorp and Landi collections (pp. 50, 52) were all-embracing. Martin Dorp took his Strasburg treasury of 1513 almost entirely from Phaedrus; Landi's four hundred fables were Dorp rearranged. Only a few early editions were meant just as school books, and only later were pictures expressly intended to help children read the texts.

English school *Aesops*, usually founded on Dorp, were mere language manuals, with the notable exception of a translation in plain language by the spelling reformer William Bullokar: *Aeşopz Fablż in Tru Ortŏgraphy with Grammar-notz* (1585). Caxton's version, in Darton's view still the best for children today, was not intended primarily for the young, but educationalists such as Brinsley and Locke considered fables an essential ingredient of moral instruction. The pioneering schoolmaster John Brinsley turned Aesop into a children's book for use in grammar schools (1617, 1624). He saw fables not just as lessons in accidence but as worth reading for pleasure and self-improvement. The educational reformer Comenius realised the efficacy of visual aids, but it was Locke who recommended pictures of animals as bait, claiming that character was more important than learning. An almost unknown fable-book of 1703, supervised or written by Locke, has four pages of 'sculptures', each containing sixteen tiny square cuts of animals (see also pp. 4, 22). John Newbery, the eminent and eminently successful children's publisher, treated fables more lightly though with an inevitable discursiveness. His much reprinted *Fables in Verse for the Improvement of the Young and the Old*, by Abraham Aesop Esq. (1757), compiled with Christopher Smart (?), introduces 'Woglog the great Giant' – but Newbery is more in evidence than Aesop.

From Caxton to Croxall, fabulists have claimed to write for the young, some with little justification. Among the 'polite' or refined gift-book *Aesops*, it is often

THE FROG AND THE OX.

OPPOSITE: 'The Frog and the Ox'
by Charles Henry Bennett, from *The Fables of Aesop and Others*, 1857 (see pp. 98-9)

BELOW: 'The Wind and the Sun'
by Walter Crane, from *The Baby's Own Aesop*, 1887 (see pp. 108-9)

THE WIND & THE SUN

THE WIND and the Sun had a bet,
The wayfarers' cloak which should get:
Blew the Wind – the cloak clung:
Shone the Sun – the cloak flung
Showed the Sun had the best of it yet.

· TRUE · STRENGTH · IS · NOT · BLUSTER ·

11

hard to distinguish between adult and juvenile editions (see pp. 16-17, 54). Ogilby and L'Estrange addressed their handsome albums to both young and elegant, finding school versions 'unworthy'. L'Estrange like his near-contemporary Locke saw the youthful mind as 'blank paper'. The first to state explicitly that children are fond of 'little stories', he attached much more significance to text and moral than to pictures, which he regarded as a mere tool for schoolmasters. It is ironic that L'Estrange, who was first printed without pictures, is now so often illustrated. In France, lay schools were quick to replace the traditional religious morals with those of La Fontaine; his fables were popular with both young and old, and learnt at an early age.

After Newbery, changing attitudes towards youth - the discovery of children as individuals and the desire of a new mercantile middle class for education - meant that fables became genuine reading for the young (though soon forced to share the honours with fairy tales, now respectable once more). A century earlier it had been fashionable – and commercial – to invent original fables for adults. Now, after a time-lag, new fables were written for children – again only loosely based on folklore: Mrs Trimmer's *Ladder to Learning* (1789 *etc*) and William Godwin's *Fables Ancient and Modern* (1805) with plates by Mulready (?) which imitate Dodsley in form if not content (see endpapers). More amusing and idiosyncratic are *Old Friends in a New Dress* (1807) by R. S. Sharpe, whose limericks inspired Lear, and Jefferys Taylor's *Aesop in Rhyme, with some Originals* (1820-21). With Romanticism, fables moved to the fringes of literature, regarded as animal stories rather than as a separate species, and relegated to reading books. A sentimental religiosity was all the rage, typified in the enthusiastically-received work of Wilhelm Hey (p. 90). Hey and his illustrator Speckter used pictures as a prop to memory: John Locke would have approved. But in spite of their titles these were improving verses rather than authentic fables. By the end of the century fables were banished to an underground existence, skulking in anthologies. For fifty years even reading books had few fables – but since the 1960s juvenile editions have flourished again.

Till quite recently educational psychologists considered young children almost incapable of abstract reasoning and logical thought, and of assimilating the meaning of a fable (Doderer) – but El Lissitzky comments that children can manipulate abstraction actively while conditioned adults must be content with passive enjoyment (*Of Two Squares* 1922). It is wrong to present fables only as stories about animals: even the youngest child is capable of thinking about what he sees or hears. The briskness of the traditional fables is suited to a brief attention span – and besides, to the young or childlike, talking animals are more interesting than human beings! Joseph Jacobs remarked: 'The more they observe animals, the more they understand men', and La Fontaine that fables give children their first knowledge of animal types and so of human types – and consequently of themselves.

History of the Illustrations

When Prometheus wanted to created mankind, he took the dominant quality of each beast, and from such diverse parts he made our kind; this work we call the microcosm. And so these fables are a picture in which each of us finds his portrait.

La Fontaine: *Préface*, 1668

Of all ancient literary forms fables have inspired the most continuous and varied pictorial tradition, reflecting in miniature the wider history of book illustration. With its dramatic simplicity of action and lack of circumstantial detail or psychological complexity, a fable lends itself to illustration. The texts are universally familiar, yet their literary merit not such that it inhibits attempts at visual explanation. There is no one definitive text of Aesop nor, apart from Gheeraerts, has one illustrator set a standard for comparison. Independent of time and place, a fable subject gives free rein to the artist. Ideally the picture should explain both story and moral; in practice most artists have chosen to illustrate the action, usually at its climax. The more situational a fable, the more completely it can be told in a single picture – but conversational fables with dialogue rather than activity present a greater problem. Some similarity of approach is unavoidable because of the nature of fables: brief, unadorned, allowing a limited number of possibilities – but there is scope for choice in the most straightforward fable. Some features can be underlined, others ignored. The drama of the story is most immediately attractive; the moral has rarely affected the illustration. Pictures can provoke more vivid and lasting memories than words, which the exceptional interpreter will complement and enrich.

Certain fables have always been singled out for visual treatment, often in other media than paper and printing ink. 'The Fox and the Stork', pictured on vases and tombstones from Ur to Rome, was the most frequently reproduced fable of the Middle Ages. 'The Fox and the Crow', more rarely seen, is embroidered on the borders of the Bayeux Tapestry – the first known English representations of Aesop. Fable motifs were kept alive in illuminated initials or in Gothic capitals and misericords: details of the Ulm choir pews are repeated in the *Ulm Aesop*. The copper creatures in the labyrinth at Versailles (pp. 60-1) reappear in a book. Coalport china, Chelsea porcelain and Minton tiles were decorated with fable subjects, evidence of a continuing popularity. Aesop appears on reliefs and murals, biscuit tins of the 1880s and a 1922 film cartoon by Paul Terry. On paper, fables might be reproduced singly or small selections of pictures issued as independent decoration – but some so-called fable representations turn out to be merely ornamental animal figures.

In the past the picture had to be instantly recognisable, however much the texts might vary: the image was sacred, at once a symbol and a reminder. Similar 'motifs' – the attitudes and relationships of the characters (Hodnett 1979) – constantly recur, often detectable only by a trained eye. Just as the bare bones of the texts kept their integrity, so too did visual patterns (travelling separately) stay remarkably constant. All early printed fables are dependent on series in illuminated manuscripts, and striking parallels have been found between mediaeval and classical illustrations. A continuous tradition seems likely from ancient times. This continuity is explored in Edward Hodnett's study of the descent and interdependence of fable motifs: *Aesop in England* (1979), and also by Küster (1970). Erber examines 'The Fox and the Raven' (1980/81) and Bodemann 'The Dog and the Meat' (Wolfenbüttel 1983). Dr Mary Hobbs has followed the 'Ant and Fly' iconography, from Caxton's image reversed in 1501 through Ogilby to Bewick. 'The Ant and the Grasshopper' (pp. 92-3) is another case in point, as is the fable of the two pots. Included in *Ecclesiasticus* ('for how agree the kettle and the earthen pot together'), it provides a design for Boner's *Edelstein* and one of eight fable motifs in Alciati's *Emblematum liber* of 1531. The iconography remains virtually unchanged over the next one hundred and fifty years. Centuries later, Rackham's pots are swimming (as in Alciati) but Grandville's are companions on the road (pp. 28, 89).

Fables imposed as many limitations on the artist as they allowed him freedoms. Not only respect for tradition but avarice, inertia, lack of time and editor's instructions – and even feelings of impotence in the face of previous excellence – acted as curbs on the individual imagination. Marcus Gheeraerts' fable series is exceptional in begetting a long procession of copies. No stigma was attached to plagiarism, and designs were regarded as fair game at least until the seventeenth century (pp. 55, 68-9). Besides, early illustrations were mainly anonymous and no *Aesop* before 1531 bears a signature. Few mediaeval artists signed their own work – except in hidden places. Modern ideas of personal fame were alien to them, and their creative powers, even in the secular field, were dedicated to the greater glory of God.

Imitation varied from mechanical copying to inspired reconstructions. Wood blocks were valuable property and much borrowed: Zainer's were re-used by Bämler

OPPOSITE: 'The Cock and the Pearl'
by Kanō Tomonobu, from *Choix de fables de La Fontaine*,
Tokyo 1894 (see pp. 110-11)

BELOW: 'The Jay in Peacock's Plumes'
by André Hellé, from *Fables de La Fontaine*, 1922 (see
pp. 114-15)

of Augsburg (the V&A's Sorg *Aesop* bears his label). A skilful cutter could achieve a near-facsimile reproduction – whereas etching was usually done by the artist himself, making imitation much harder. Elements from two models might be combined, or designs adapted to the changing page (see p. 49); Krafft actually traced Gheeraerts' designs, varying the backgrounds (p. 69).

The first Western dated illustrated book was Boner's *Edelstein*, chief source for Zainer's *Ulm Aesop*: the first fable-book with pictures in Germany. Caxton based the cuts for his *Aesop* – the third English illustrated book – on Lyons copies of the Zainer blocks taken from the Sorg edition. His series, less successful than expected, was not part of the line of descent to Barlow. France initiated a change of style which took root in the Netherlands and in Italy (p. 42). A leading printer in the 1540s was Janot of Paris, whose *Aesop* was parent to a long run of little books printed in Lyons from 1547 with Bernard Salomon's much-copied cuts. Designs by Solis modelled on Salomon appear in a pirated Frankfurt edition (Feyerabend, 1566); these popular cuts gave rise to a succession of imitations contemporary with but largely independent of Gheeraerts. By 1600 there were nearly seven hundred fable editions, more than a third with pictures. Text was valued more highly than illustration in Germany and Flanders, but Italy and France preferred pictures.

The earliest dated *Aesop* (Domenico di Vivaldi, Mondovì, 1476) had rudimentary metal cuts and no successors. The chief source for fable illustration in Italy was Accio Zucco's 1479 *Verona Aesop*, printed by Alvise; it influenced only slightly the more celebrated *Naples Aesop* of 1485 (pp. 36-7). Peculiar to Italy were illustrated editions containing only Aesop's *Life* – first included in the *Naples Aesop* (see also p. 78). Faerno's fables (pp. 44-5) seem always to have been illustrated, and Pirro Ligorio's series the only etched one to predate Gheeraerts, whose outstanding Aesop designs head a new age of naturalism. From the sixteenth century an increasing desire to understand nature more objectively demanded more accurate representation. Since animals play such a leading part in fables, their treatment is a critical aspect of fable illustration. Gheeraerts was one of the first Europeans to specialise in zoological drawing, and to set his animals in real and luxuriant landscapes – even if occasionally at the expense of the action. His designs to de Dene's *De Warachtighe Fabulen der Dieren* (1567), the work of his maturity, were imitated more or less faithfully from 1578 to 1786 and can be traced as far as Bewick.

On Gheeraerts' Netherlands focussed the emblematic fable development (see pp. 42-3). Allegory is a dead art today, but at that time emblematic pictures were understood by all. The earliest emblem book consisting entirely of fables was Corrozet's *Fables du tresancien Esope* (see above and pp. 42, 52); de Dene's was only the second work of this kind. Many emblem books contain pictures of animals: the borderline between the two types becomes blurred. Corrozet derived his designs from Brant's Basel *Aesop* of 1501 and so indirectly from the *Ulm Aesop*; Perret and others took their mise-en-page from Corrozet. Perret's *Aesop* (pp. 48-9) was printed together with emblem books by Plantin of Antwerp, from where both picture and text spread all over Europe. Individual pictures became symbol-bearers and were used as emblems, while 'emblematic' fables such as Alciati's 'The Two Pots' (p. 23) joined the Aesopic tradition. The coexistence of emblem books with emblematic fable-books ensured an amazing variety in the genre; throughout the sixteenth century additions were made, but the basic three-layered structure never changes. With an emblem the picture is primary but static, whereas a fable picture must represent the action. Emblematic fable illustration did not thrive for long because fables are self-sufficient, able to exist without picture or riddle.

The language of emblem and allegory came into its own in programmatic title pages or frontispieces, often portraying Aesop with a group of fable-animals. The conspicuous title page of the *Ulm Aesop* is an early example, its 'hieroglyphs' referring to Aesop's life, whereas in Triller's *Neue Aesopische Fabeln* (1740) Fable covers Truth with a veil bearing scenes from the fables. Gheeraerts represents man as the crown of creation but still dependent on nature (1567); Cleyn again shows Aesop with supporting cast (a theme repeated by Kredel in 1966). The title page to Richardson's fables gives Aesop a child's face, evidence of a new approach.

In spite of an unsettled political climate the Baroque period produced some outstanding books, flamboyant or formal and comparable in size, costliness and exclusiveness with the modern 'livre d'artiste'. Great artists were now participating in book art - but illustrations of a high calibre appeared in England only after the Restoration. The two outstanding English *Aesops* of the century were both etched reinterpretations of Gheeraerts. The first was Hollar's elegant folio of 1665, financed by a lottery (pp. 56-7); the second was Barlow's trilingual *Aesop* (pp. 62-3).

Etched book decoration was then still relatively rare, but the two artists had long been etchers before simultaneously turning to fable illustration. Hollar - imported, like Cleyn (pp. 54-5) - created virtually a new art form in England: 'printed book illustrations as works of independent charm' (Hodnett 1979). Though his animals are rather stiff, he imitated Gheeraerts in 'faithfully rendered costumes, interiors, rustic cottages, and stately castles', surpassing him in the 'decorative backdrops of ancient trees, majestic mountains, and spacious harbors' and drawing recognisable views of places he had visited. Barlow was the first Englishman to make a speciality of zoological illustration. He surveys the scene from an animal's viewpoint, as the unknown artist of the *Verona Aesop* adopts a 'low Mantegnesque eye-level' (*TLS* 1973). The main source for Bewick, Barlow had some influence also on Dodsley's designs, on Oudry (through a French edition) and above all on Kirkall's metal cuts (pp. 84-5) - responsible for Croxall's eventual if temporary triumph over his unillustrated rival L'Estrange. Barlow's motifs look down from old inn signs - 'the last symbolic animals to gain currency' (Clark: *Animals and Men* 1977).

France, having set the fashion for 'literary' fables, now moved into the vanguard of fable illustration. New fables inspired new designs, and even designs for traditional fables depended less on pre-existing models; also, artists had become sensitive to accusations of plagiarism. La Fontaine so integrated his diverse sources that his interpreters had no need to look over their shoulders - but the first of all, François Chauveau, did not work in a vacuum. La Fontaine had shown him Solis' cuts, and he even borrows Roman ruins from Gheeraerts. In the eighteenth century a smaller, more economical format was preferred, in keeping with delicate Rococo confections such as Gillot's vignetted headpieces to La Motte (1719) and Marillier's to Dorat (p. 75). Some French publishers still printed large-format books - already an anachronism. Oudry's four-volume *La Fontaine*, the 'Paris edition' (pp. 72-3), was the handsomest and most massive of its century, embellished with two hundred and seventy-six plates and almost as many vignettes. Like Marillier's *Contes* of La Fontaine it was funded by financiers (and by the King). Engravings after Gheeraerts and Oudry served as models for artists working in other media; Oudry's plates were re-engraved by Gabriel Huquier the Elder as '*Livres d'animaux*'.

OPPOSITE: 'The Two Pots'
by Arthur Rackham, from *Aesop's Fables*, 1912 (see
pp. 112-13)

BELOW: 'The Stag Quenching his Thirst'
by Willi Harwerth, from *Klingspor Kalender für das Jahr
1933* (see pp. 120-1)

Germany experienced a mainly literary development; more common than complete series were designs for selected or single fables, as in Chodowiecki's almanacs. Since money was in shorter supply here, fabulists appeared in cheap editions. England still produced fine fable-books: Gay (pp. 70-1), Bewick (pp. 86-7), and Northcote's illustrations to his own fables (1828) - inspired by boyhood copying of pictures from Aesop. The end of the century brought a new freedom of interpretation (though something of their forebears still shows in Bewick and Blake). By the 1830s illustrations of time-honoured texts proliferated and recognised artists again took part, but original fables, unless for the young, rarely had pictures. Few attempts were made to illustrate every fable; editions became smaller, reflecting the artist's personal choice - apart from the grand-scale conceptions of Grandville and Doré (pp. 88-9, 100-1). In these great interpreters of La Fontaine the two strands of mid-nineteenth century fable illustration unite: naturalism and caricature.

Grandville often inserts a scene from everyday life behind the main action: the 'archaic multiple-event approach' (Hodnett 1979) of Cleyn and van Vianen, who combine several episodes in one picture (pp. 10, 55). Doré and Caldecott show juxtaposed but separate scenes, Bennett only the human story. His animals are not human types but men in animal masks - a device too of Lear and Tenniel's *Alice* - and the mediaeval satirists. Doré returns to La Fontaine's pessimism, and to his awareness that the smallest creatures leave the most lasting impression. Animals were now viewed in a more sympathetic light, and strenuous efforts made to encourage humane attitudes in children. At the same time, an urge to get exact likenesses of living things on to paper was actively indulged by amateurs and professionals alike. This new exploration of nature was well catered for in the sensitive naturalism of 'Sixties' artists such as Weir (pp. 104–5).

Bennett, Griset and Tenniel followed Grandville but Tenniel's creatures, natural like Weir's, contrast with the modern applications of Bennett's barbed and worldly fables (pp. 20, 97, 99, 103). Griset's 'coal-tip countryside' (Blount) and Walter Crane's stylised *Baby's Own Aesop*, more adult than babyish, reveal the underside of Victorian life. Gentler Biedermeier designs by Richter and Speckter were favourites in England as in Germany. By the early twentieth century standards in fable illustration for children had dropped and garish colours were the rule, always excepting Heighway (for Jacobs, 1894), Detmold (1909) and Rackham (pp. 28, 113). Beatrix Potter's delicate watercolours (see p. 18) are reminiscent of Caldecott, whom she much admired; her vignetted rural settings bring us back to Bewick.

Editions for adults were still scarce, but from the 1920s there was a resurgence in fable illustration, now stylistically independent of its forbears but once more for the rich – superior coffee-table books. In England the private presses catered for aficionados of fine printing. Attracting a different but again a limited market were the 'livre d'artiste' *La Fontaines*. Their godparent was Gogol's *Les Âmes mortes* with engravings by Chagall – commissioned in 1923 but published only in 1948. Bonnard's drawings for La Fontaine were never published; Derain's, prepared for Vollard, only in 1950 and Chagall's (p. 125) only in 1952. The finest 'livre d'artiste' fable-book, it had a seminal influence on others – precious and exclusive hybrids halfway between book and picture. Among the private press wood engravers Agnes Miller Parker (p. 119) stands out for the vitality of her animals and her three-dimensional effects of light and movement. Rudolph Ruzicka illustrated his *La Fontaine* (1930) with copper engravings, the first in an American book; Gooden's designs (p. 123) are in archaic style and the same medium. In the 1940s the Swiss artist Hans Fischer did exquisite calligraphic lithographs, also for La Fontaine (see too p. 83). Other distinguished twentieth-century interpreters are Artzybasheff (1933), Masyutin (1938) and Eberlein (1972). In the tradition of Busch and Thurber, Wolfdietrich Schnurre illustrated his own fables (1957).

Aesthetic and structural criteria have triumphed: picture need no longer explain text and didacticism has become irrelevant. The illustration may symbolise or synthesise the fable, but is often too abstract to be easily understood. Instead, text is needed to explain picture. The composition may be reduced to a group of static figures in confrontation or, as in Lurçat (1950) and Krol (pp. 32, 129), to a single figure enclosed in its own consciousness (Riese-Hubert). Without detail or emotion an artist fails to capture the atmosphere, however beautiful and striking his design, and the intrinsic drama is lost. But fable-animals have always been symbols: is abstraction in fact more appropriate than actualisation in fable illustration?

Many contemporary artistic movements have been reflected through the art of the book. Artists today prefer to tackle familiar fables; illustrations as well as texts have been revived since World War II (Doré, Grandville, fifteenth-century woodcuts). Perhaps the realism of the early cuts – and of their modern followers – is closest to the essential Aesop. Elaborate fine-art products of the seventeenth and eighteenth centuries can appear cold and formal, far removed from Aesop's primitive directness. Biedermeier naturalism seems sentimental, the avant-garde approach too rarified. Attempts to condescend to children can lead to an empty prettiness – but an exaggerated naturalism might elicit an over-compassionate response (Doderer 1971). Fable heroes should not be too like real animals, or we shall be tempted to forget 'the bitter truth of the fables': that the world is imperfect and unjust.

Fables and Society

Fables have always served as a microcosm of the world – La Fontaine's 'petit monde'. Though part of a less structured society than Reynard the Fox, each fable animal has its specific status, demonstrated in mode of speech or style of address. A fable normally involves two actors and a confrontation, even a conflict. So obviously do the stories reflect human power struggles that, not surprisingly, they have often been adopted for teaching politics to princes. La Fontaine's first and last books were dedicated to royal children, and Gay's earlier fables 'invented to amuse' a little Duke. The classical scholar Hoogstraten edited a de luxe *Phaedrus* – suitably elevated in style – for the young Prince of Nassau (pp. 10-11).

Fables had a rather different political rôle in mediaeval Europe, where they travelled in company with a related form, the epigrammatic *Spruchdichtung*. As covert propaganda for the oppressed, emblematic fables were appropriated by the 'Rederijker' (p. 46), a Calvinist group powerful in political and intellectual life. Inflammatory broadsheets contained fable illustrations based on the widely-disseminated copper engravings of Gheeraerts who himself had fled persecution, his ransom paid by Plantin. During long-drawn-out religious wars, the Netherlands suffered under the yoke of France. Louis XIV is lampooned in the lion and courtiers of de Hooghe's *Esopus in Europa* (1700-01), a collection of pamphlets parodying Aesopic fable. With Ogilby, English fables for the first time double as agitatory literature; L'Estrange, dubbed 'Dog Towzer', was one of our earliest partisan journalists. The great popularity of fables in nineteenth-century France kept alive the tradition of animals as human substitutes. Russian writers have long used 'Aesopian' devices (the old emblematic method) to outwit censors and facilitate reading between the lines (*TLS* 25 Oct 1985, p. 1204). Though political caricature is the most characteristic aesthetic agitprop of the present century, forward-looking artists have transformed the ancient symbols into images of bitter pessimism.

Literature and politics are still spiced with Aesopian allusion. In 1858 Trollope's Dr Fillgrave with his efforts at magnificence evoked the Frog and the Ox. In 1984 the heroine of Anita Brookner's *Hôtel du Lac* speculates about the Hare and the Tortoise, cynically convinced that Aesop meant to console the meeker 'tortoise market' and that in fact the Hare always finishes first. Only certain fables are remembered, as often for their actors as for their morals: politicians and letters to *The Times* still cite the Hawks and the Doves. Such unconscious, automatic expressions have been inherited from a stockpile of sayings, 'those tremendous truths that are called truisms' (Chesterton). Fables are now as hackneyed as proverbs.

Society is still in need of Aesop's subtle reminders. Human weaknesses have hardly changed since his time, nor have animal stereotypes – in our mind's eye wolves are still fierce and lambs defenceless, and the 'revolt of a sheep' (Balzac) still inconceivable. Fables like myths are 'objective equivalents of every possible human situation' (Michael Innes: *The Weight of the Evidence*); they confront the

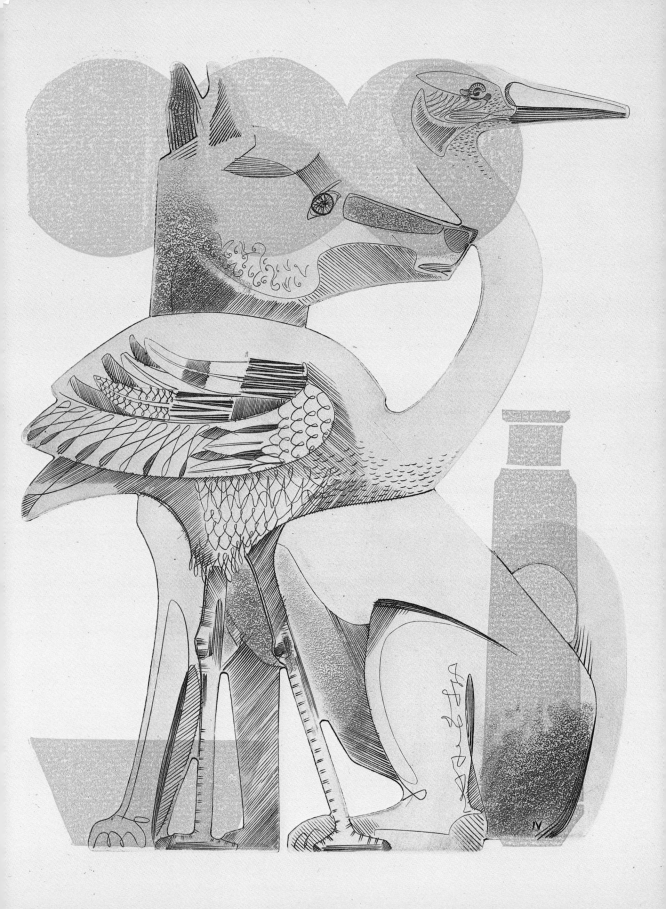

problems of coexistence, their morals are unchangeable axioms – yet one can always find fables offering contradictory advice. The same paradoxes occur in the Bible. These ambiguities were not inherently perverse but formulated out of experience of the world. The message of fables is a practical but hard-headed and often selfish one. 'It is in some sort Natural to be a Knave' (L'Estrange), and it is acceptable to repay trickery in kind if in self-defence. Even villainy arouses a grudging admiration, if allied to ingenuity. The 'archetypal deceiver' Reynard, who represents our worst self (Blount), inevitably turns into a sympathetic character, almost always successful (according to Varty) but often represented visually as a loser.

There is little pity to spare for losers, in the early fables at least. Force and cunning frequently prevail and advantage is taken of the weak. Rough justice is the rule, imposed by nature or by fate. The strong are always right and the fittest survive – but success may be short-lived. Honesty or patience are occasionally acknowledged; good turns are recommended but not necessarily rewarded; the weak but wily may overcome. In general though, fable characters have an eye to the main chance, and not much genuine kindness. The original fables were entirely secular, even if they later lent themselves to the purposes of preachers who realised their entertainment potential (Jesus is said never to have told humorous stories, however). Till the nineteenth century compassion hardly intervenes. If the Christian qualities of humility and meekness are ever advocated in fables, it is as a sensible compromise or a means to an end. Nowadays such an approach might seem unfashionably middle-of-the-road, although in these times of cold war and détente an expedient one.

In fables taken at their face value and not used for subversive ends, the established order is respected, superior strength usually justified and social climbing discouraged. Treachery has always threatened the fabric of society: the position of the powerful must be maintained and current norms respected. 'All animals are equal, but some are more equal than others' (Orwell: *Animal Farm*). Fables demonstrate a fatalistic resignation to the inevitable by those condemned to a place for ever below the salt – and on another level, an understanding of human nature. The perpetual confrontations of the fable world are not only external but within. Opposing sides of our nature are at war: our passions rebel at the prudent dictates of conscience, and our scruples cannot curb our pride.

It would be a mistake to become too solemn on the subject of fables – intended after all to make people laugh as much as think. Such comedies were offspring of Greek peasant celebrations, telling not of the powerful nor of the wicked but of the ridiculous (Eco: *The Name of the Rose*). By exposing human frailties they achieved the catharsis of laughter, advocated by Aristotle as a thought-provoking force for good. To make people laugh at the truth is to 'make truth laugh'.

For *Children* must be Ply'd with *Idle Tales*, and *Twittle-Twattles*; and betwixt *Jest* and *Earnest*, Flatter'd, and Cajol'd, into a *Sense*, and *Love* of their *Duty*.

L'Estrange: *To the Reader*, 1699

OPPOSITE: 'The Fox and the Stork' by Abram Krol, from *Jean de La Fontaine: XXIV fables*, 1959 (see pp. 128–9)

1. OF THE FOXE AND OF THE RAYSYNS

He is not wyse: that desyreth to have a thynge whiche he may not have: As reciteth this fable Of a foxe: whiche loked and beheld the raysyns that grewe upon an hyghe vyne: the whiche raysyns he moche desyred for to ete them.

And whanne he sawe that none he myght gete: he torned his sorowe in to Ioye: and sayd these raysyns ben sowre: and yf I had some I wold not ete them: And therfore this fable sheweth that he is wyse: whiche fayneth not to desyre that thynge the whiche he may not have.

Caxton (after Steinhöwel), 1483/84
as in the *Gregynog Aesop*, 1931

Vita Esopi fabulatoris clarissimi e greco latina P, Rimiciu facta.... [Mit] seinen fabeln von doctore heinrico steinhöwel geteütschet [and with fables from Romulus, partly versified by the Anonymus Neveleti, fables selected from Avianus and others, and the *Facetiae* of Poggio Bracciolini]. Fol. [Augsburg, Anton Sorg, *c.* 1479] 1474-1895

The extraordinary diversity of the Germanic fable world is met between the covers of one book: Steinhöwel's monumental two-language compendium, the '*Ulm Aesop*' (Zainer, 1476/77). Steinhöwel had studied medicine in Padua, where he came into contact with Humanist thought – and accordingly incorporated recently discovered Greek traditions and contemporary Renaissance 'short stories' into the wide variety of mediaeval sources available to him. He included Aesop's *Life*, an Eastern fable of Petrus Alfonsus, and Poggio Bracciolini's *Liber facetiorum* (1471), a collection of jests and *fabliaux* including 'The Miller, Son and Ass'. Steinhöwel's purpose was to offer the Latin fables in new clothing, providing them with texts in the vernacular and with illustrations (which relate to the German translation). For this he earned Luther's criticism that his fables were more entertaining than useful.

The *Ulm Aesop*, contrary to popular belief, was not the first printed fable-book, nor was it the only anthology to contain fables, but it obviously answered a demand and immediately had greater success than its rivals. Among the most celebrated editions based on Zainer was Sorg's of *c.* 1479, again a product of South-West Germany where there was a thriving community of printers. Through its French and English translations (Caxton's in particular) the fables became familiar throughout Europe.

Steinhöwel's was one of the earliest illustrated editions of the fifteenth century. Its designs were dependent on various manuscript sources (including the eleventh-century *Romulus* of the monk Ademar), the Netherlandish woodcut tradition, and – for half the cycle – on the primitive outline cuts in Boner's *Der Edelstein* (Pfister of Bamberg, 1461). This was the first printed collection of Aesopic fables and the first dated illustrated book, its designs taken from lost originals. *Der Edelstein* was already well-known in manuscript versions when Boner's edition appeared; it was an important model for fable illustration in Northern Europe. With a bold, expressive economy of line and strong characterisation, the series is a convincing piece of animal type-casting.

Of all late mediaeval fable designs, Sorg's were the most influential and the most often copied – though cut after the *Ulm Aesop* by an unidentified artist or artists and so derivative rather than innovative. These illustrations were much admired by

William Morris, who had not seen Boner's *Edelstein.* Never placed at the top of the page, and open above as if to fit specially designed frames (see also the *Naples Aesop*, p. 37), they show one particular instant in the story. Only the title page was full-length. As in the *Edelstein* (Hodnett 1979) their jagged outlines are 'restricted to the chief actors, minimum accessories, bumpy terrain, and a tree or two' with vestigial leaves. The artist, in a more studied attempt at naturalism, has succeeded in contriving unusually lifelike animals: only the exotic creatures retain a heraldic formality characteristic of the time. This series was directly and indirectly the chief source for Aesopic fable illustration in Europe for at least three centuries.

2. OF THE WULVES AND OF THE SHEEP

Whanne Men have a good hede: and a good defensour: or a good Capitayne: men oughte not to leve hym: for he that leveth hym repenteth hym after ward of hit: as to us reherceth this fable: Of the sheep whiche had werre and descension with the wolves: And by cause that the wulves made to stronge werre ageynst the sheep: the shepe thenne tooke for theyr help the dogges: and the whethers also: And thenne was the bataylle of the sheep so grete and so stronge: & fought so vygorously ageynst the wolves that they put them to flyght.

And whanne the wolves sawe the strengthe of theyr adversaryes: they sent an ambassade toward the sheep for to trete the pees with them: the whiche Ambassade sayd to the sheep in this maner: yf ye wylle gyve us the dogges: we shalle swere unto yow oure feythe: that we shalle never kepe ne hold werre ageynst yow: And the sheep ansuerd: yf ye wylle gyve us your fayth: we shalle be content: And thus they made pees to gyder: but the wulves kyld the dogges: whiche were capytayns and protectours of the sheep: And the dogges dyde but lytyll hurte to the wulves: wherfore whanne the lytyl and yong wulves were growen in theyr age: they came of eche part and countrey: and assembled them to gyder: and all of one accord and wylle sayd to theyr aunscestres and faders: we must ete up alle the sheep: And theyr faders ansuerd thus to them: we have made pees with them: Nevertheles the yonge wolves brake the pees and ranne fyersly upon the sheep: and theyr faders wente after them:

And thus by cause that the sheep had delyverd the dogges to the wolves: the whiche were theyr capitayns: and that they had none that kepte them: they were all eten and devoured of the wulves: Therfore hit is good to kepe well his capytayne: whiche may at a nede gyve socor and helpe: For a trewe frend is oftyme better at a nede than a Royalme: For yf the sheep had kepte the love of the dogges: the wolves had never devoured them: wherfore it is a sure thynge to kepe wel the love of his protectour and good frende.

Caxton (after Steinhöwel), 1483/84
as in the *Gregynog Aesop*, 1931

[The *Aesopus moralisatus* of Francesco del Tuppo, the fables translated from the Anonymus Neveleti, the *Vita* from Rinuccio. In Latin and Italian.] Fol.(imperfect) [Naples, by the Germani fidelissimi for Francesco del Tuppo, 1485]   14.iv.1866

Best-known of all Italian fable-books was the '*Naples Aesop*'. Its eighty-eight illus-trations descended from the accomplished but more rudimentary woodcuts of Accio Zucco's *Verona Aesop* (Alvise, 1479), possibly by the miniature-painter Liberale da Verona (see also p. 26). From this edition all early Italian fable illustrations were derived: the German tradition succeeding Zainer's Ulm series was not to reach Italy for another century. Various theories are held about the 'Master of the *Naples Aesop*'. The heterogeneous designs are part Nordic, part Spanish; some may be copies of compositions by the Master E. S. As in the *Ulm Aesop* the dramatic central event takes precedence over background detail, but here the elements of each composition are more consciously arranged on the page. Spatial relationships have been handled with typical Italian skill, though the initial cutter – apparently of the Strasburg school – must have followed a South Italian manuscript example.

So sharp and sure is the work that these illustrations have been taken for metal cuts. Presented with confident, accomplished draughtsmanship, flexibility of line and a deep perspective, the figures engage as if on a stage where the sets are strange flowering trees.

The magnificence of these pictures is considerably enhanced by their elaborate borders and entablatures, each taking up at least one-third of the printed surface. Inspired by Hispano-Moresque ornament, they were designed separately and executed by a different hand. At the head of the illustration reproduced above is one of three recurring classical motifs: in this instance two pygmies in combat, mounted on mythical beasts.

The 'Aesopus moralisatus' (see p. 14), which existed in thirteen textual variants, was a comparatively small selection of fables in metric adaptations from the 'Anonymus Neveleti', whose verse collection was one of the main sources for the Middle Ages (see pp. 14–15, 118). Francesco del Tuppo translated his sixty-six Latin verse fables after Macho's version into Italian prose, adding – probably with didactic intent – allegorical, moral and historical commentaries.

Opposite is another, longer excerpt from Caxton – still the standard English Aesop in 1485 – scattered with his characteristic pairs of words or 'doublets'.

3. THE RIVAL FISHES

Of the Carp, the Grayling, the Turtle and the Dolphin

The river fish were celebrating in some solemnity after a banquet, swimming about together and tranquil with repletion. But the Carp began to disturb their festivities, raising himself up and saying: Not only am I the worthiest of all but my flesh is inexpressibly perfumed and delicate. I was nurtured neither in ditches and swamps nor yet in marshes. I was reared in great Lake Garda, and on account of that I deserve to be supreme among you. When the Grayling [*temallus* or *?temolo*] heard this he leapt up in indignation and said: What you are claiming is not true. I am superior to you in scent and savour. He who may taste me has found a treasure indeed. If you are a denizen of Lake Garda – which is tantamount to being a marsh-dweller – why then *I* come from the wide rivers. So their festivities were disturbed by quarrelling and strife, since some supported one contestant and some the other, and they were about to tear one another apart on the spot. In the meantime a certain learned and ancient Turtle [*turtur* or turtur-fish] spoke out, saying: Brothers, it is not good to fight for the sake of vain braggarts. I do not praise myself, although I am worthy of praise, for it is written: *Let another man praise thee, and not thine own mouth* [Proverbs XXVII, 2], since all such praise defiles the mouth which speaks it. Therefore it is better for those who praise themselves to pay suit to the judge of the seas, that is the Dolphin, who is righteous and God-fearing and will try this case justly. Her exhortation pleased them all, and the two contestants at once proceeded to the Dolphin's court, informing him of all these matters and flattering themselves as much as they were able. The Dolphin said to them: My little sons, I have never seen you before, since you lie hidden in the rivers while I dive among the fruits of the sea. Because of this I can hardly pronounce judgement unless I first try you. With these words he gave a leap and gobbled them up, saying: No one should praise himself at the expense of his fellows with impunity.

Many people continually praise themselves and applaud their own actions, wishing to lord it over others in their vanity and pride. But the righteous and humble criticise themselves. And as G[regory] says: *We descend by self-exaltation and ascend by humility.* Whence Job XXXI in the same vein: *If my mouth hath kissed my hand: This also were an iniquity to be punished by the judge.* He who praises his own works is kissing his own hand. Luke XVII teaches us the same truth, saying: *When ye shall have done all those things which are commanded you, say, We are unprofitable servants: we have done that which was our duty to do.*

For the story goes that the birds found a nest scented with roses and other flowers, and the eagle, king of the birds, decreed that this nest would be given to the noblest bird, and summoned all the birds of the air to a meeting, asking them to name the most beautiful of all. The cuckoo answered Cuckoo. And again the eagle asked which was the mightiest bird, and he answered Cuckoo. And the eagle said angrily: Wretched Cuckoo, you always extol yourself and never praise others, and yet you are not the most beautiful bird, nor the swiftest, nor the strongest, nor are you a fine singer, but your cry is always the same. And therefore I pronounce

sentence, condemning you to have neither this nest nor any other as your own. And so to this day they continually praise themselves, and always sing Cuckoo.

A. S. H.

Destructoriũ vitiorum ex similitudinũ creaturaru3 exemplorum appropriatiõe per modu3 dyalogi. auctoritatũq3 sacrarum. scripturarũ philosophorum et poetarum: cõstructoriumq3 virtutum. [Dialogus creaturarum.] 4to. (Lugd., per Claudium nourry, 1509)   12.viii.1865

The 'Dialogus creaturarum moralisatus' (c. 560), a collection of beast-tales attributed to Nicolaus Pergamenus or Maynus de Mayneriis, was first published in 1480 by Leeu of Gouda and several times reprinted. One of the choicest Dutch illustrated books, its delightfully humorous cuts are reminiscent of block book style but 'display a lightness and fantasy ... quite foreign to German work of the time' (Bland 1969). As an ancestor of the Mikrokosmos (1579) with plates conceivably by Gheeraerts (reprinted by de Jode for Plantin in 1584 as the Apologi creaturarum and, with Flemish text, as Jan Moerman's De Cleyn Werelt), its indirect influence on La Fontaine is likely.

Animal satire, in fable-books, bestiaries and the Reynard the Fox epic, was a common form of veiled social criticism in the late Middle Ages; these one hundred and twenty-two fables of the Physiologus type descend from Reynard the Fox and an Aesop of c. 1472 (Utrecht, Printer of the Speculum) by the Humanist, priest and schoolmaster Lorenzo Valla (see also p. 14). A variety of short narratives with morals – parables, proverbs, exempla (see pp. 12, 18) – found their way into fable-books or were used (in the words of Erasmus Alberus) to sweeten the bitter drink of sermons, an important vehicle in the transmission of fables especially in Northern Europe. Miscellaneous anthologies such as the Dialogus creaturarum, Ulrich von Pottenstein's Speculum sapientiae, or the Directorium humanae vitae (pp. 40-1) were indirect continuations of Aesopic tradition but had far less vitality or influence, and they were eclipsed by Steinhöwel's classic collection (p. 15).

4. THE MAN IN THE WELL

I rebuked my heart: Do you not know that the pleasures of this world are full of suffering and bring everlasting affliction. Think now, better is the bitterness of wormwood with an underlying sweetness than the sweetness which hides an enduring bitterness – better a brief time of trouble if it is followed by eternal joy and peace. I reasoned with myself thus: Do you not see that this world is full of misery, poverty, travail and adversity? Do you not know that man from the moment of his birth encounters one trouble after another? As an infant he suffers hunger and thirst, and later, daily beatings; as a young man the strife and turmoil of love; then follows anxiety about his children, lying awake tormented by dreams, and the ravages of cold, heat, snow and rain. In old age he has two servants – one called pain, the other disease – as well as grim thoughts of death which will part him from his worldly goods, his heirs, his lovely wife, his children, parents and friends, and from all worldly delights, and he must travel to a place where he knows not how he will be received. Now we see that in these times good is giving way to evil, virtue has grown weak and wickedness strong. Government is taken from the righteous and given to the wicked. Treachery wakes and truth sleeps. The tree of falsehood bears fruit and the tree of truth is barren. The way of iniquity is bright and the way of righteousness is in darkness. The wicked are exalted and good men oppressed. The noble spirit is crushed by the foot of the ignoble.

I found that man was created superior to all other creatures, yet will not restrain himself from flirting with one evil after another – which with a little wisdom he might try to avoid. I was astonished to discover that man is hindered in this because of the fleeting nature of this world's delights – the pleasures found merely through seeing, hearing, smelling, tasting, touching and feeling. And it is possible that on account of these transient pleasures man neglects his eternal soul.

Such a one we see in the man pursued by a lion who in his flight came to a deep well. He climbed down into it and clung to two little saplings growing at the edge. He set his foot on an unsteady stone, then saw in front of him four beasts with lowered heads, waiting to devour him – and when he turned his gaze from them and looked down he saw below him at the bottom of the well a fierce dragon with open mouth, ready to catch him in its jaws, and then he perceived a black mouse and a white mouse gnawing away with all their might at the two saplings by which he was supporting himself. As the man stood there in great dread, not knowing when his end might come, he saw quite near him between two stones a small honeycomb which he licked at with his tongue, and with this brief sensation of sweetness forgot both himself and the need to find a way of escaping from his torments, so that he fell and was destroyed.

I compare the well to this world, the four beasts to the four elements by which every man is brought nearer to his end, and the two saplings to the life of man; the white mouse is day and the black mouse night, continually gnawing away at man's life. The dragon stands for the grave which lies in wait for man every moment of his life, and the little honeycomb for the transient pleasures of this world which cause many a man to descend into eternal torment.

A. S. H. (slightly adapted and abridged)

Das ist das buoch der weissheit darin erlernt würt der welt lauff. [New edition of Anton von Pforre's *Buch der Beispiele der alten Weisen* or fables of Bīdpāī.] Fol. (Strassburg, durch Johannem Grienninger, 1529) .1.v.1877

Oriental fables were formerly well-known to the West and had been translated into most European languages by the seventeenth century. 'Bīdpāī', like Aesop, is an enigma and his fables of complex descent: the two main streams, Arabic and Persian, derive from the *Pañchatantra* and other Sanskrit or Hindu tales (see p. 18). The adaptation by Anton von Pforre, Court Chaplain and early Humanist, was first printed by Fyner of Urach (*c.* 1481) and had appeared in seventeen editions by 1600. It travelled down from the Arabic '*Kalila and Dimna*' (so named after its jackal narrators) by way of Johannes de Capua's *Directorium humanae vitae*, translated from the Hebrew in about 1270. The Arabic stream inspired some of the finest Arab, Persian and Indian miniature painting, but only a few woodcut editions including this example by an unknown master, with its heraldic beasts symbolic of rank. In the seventeenth and eighteenth centuries, versions deriving from the Persian '*Lights of Canopus*' were retold in France and England as *The Fables of Pilpay*, in this guise providing material for La Fontaine.

The Eastern fables comprise five frame-stories encasing amusing but didactic animal tales. As a 'mirror for princes' (see p. 31) they were always intended for rulers, in Europe being the monopoly of nobles rather than bourgeoisie.

The famous Hindu parable of the man in the well (from the *Story of Samarāditya* by Haribhadra) is narrated by a Jain monk to a prince, to persuade him of the evils of this world. Here, with appropriately modified flora and fauna, it has become an allegory of the Christian soul, embedded in a sermon. The banyan tree - symbol of salvation, and wild elephant - symbol of death, have disappeared; the python symbolising Hell has been replaced by a dragon, which is the grave.

5. DEATH AND AN OLD MAN

An *Old Man* that had Travell'd a great Way under a Huge Burden of Sticks found himself so Weary that he cast it down, and call'd upon *Death* to Deliver him from a more Miserable Life. *Death* came presently at his Call, and asked him his Bus'ness. Pray Good Sir, says he, Do me but the Favour to help me up with my Burden again.

THE MORAL

Men call upon Death, as they do upon the Devil:
When he comes they're afraid of him.

L'Estrange, 6 edn, 1714

Aesopi Phrygis fabulae elegantissimis eiconibus veras animalium species ad vivum adumbrantes. [New edition. Translated by Aldus Pius Manutius. Edited by Adam Knopff. Woodcuts mainly by Bernard Salomon.] 16mo. Lugduni, apud Ioan. Tornaesium [the Elder], 1551. 974-1896

Popular small editions of fables were printed by the de Tournes father and son from 1547 onwards, containing woodcuts by their chief illustrator Bernard Salomon. His series was partly dependent on Janot's 1542 Paris edition of Corrozet's 'emblematic' fables, whose unknown artist made a radical transition from the naïve simplicity of the relatively large German Aesop blocks to the refinement of the smaller French ones, while still using the same intrinsic ingredients. Italian influence is suggested in a new fluidity and an intentional balancing of the elements. Though the old compositions persist in the 1547 edition, apparently fresh motifs are introduced, and it is Salomon's version which is responsible for the lasting vigour of the series. The same man executed many illustrations for other Janot books, and stylistic parallels have been discovered with the decorative work of Geofroy Tory, itself similar to Venetian book illustration of the time (as in Colonna's *Hypnerotomachia Poliphili*).

Much detail is crowded into these complicated little designs, which though reproduced with great mastery seem to call for bigger blocks or the more sophisticated medium of copper engraving. The fable setting and subsidiary features have acquired their own interest, and the figures, gracefully elongated in Mannerist idiom, have become part of a vast and airy landscape.

Individual fable pictures of the more symbolic kind had served as emblematic devices since antiquity, source-material for a developing form which culminated in the prototype emblem book – Alciati's *Emblematum liber* of 1531, a key work. Emblems of the more realistic sort equally became absorbed into the fable tradition: Corrozet's (founded on Dorp) was the first emblematic fable-book and later La Fontaine was to draw on the emblem tradition. Boundaries between the two forms grew ever more confused in the Renaissance and Baroque periods.

An emblem is a puzzle picture or pictorial riddle consisting of an introductory *inscriptio* or motto (often a proverb or a single word), the illustration or *pictura* (containing devices ingeniously hiding allegorical meanings) and, finally, a *subscriptio* or interpretation – often a verse epigram. Sometimes commentaries, Biblical quotations or parallel examples were added, but this three-part structure was funda-

ligna, & mortem vt veniret inuocabat. At morte ilico adstante, & causam rogante qua se vocasset, senex ait, Vt onus hoc sublatum imponeres mihi.	τὰ ξύλα, ἢ τὸν θάνατον ἐλθῶν ἐπεκαλεῖτο. τ̃ ᾗ θανάτε εὐϑὺς ἐπιϛάντΘ,ἢ τὼ αἰτίαν πυνθανομένε δι' ἣν αὐτὸν καλοίη , ὁ γέρων ἔφη,ἵνα τὸν φόρτον τοῦτον ἄρας ἐπιϑῇς μοι.

AFFABVLATIO.

Fabula significat, omnem hominem uitæ studiosum esse , & licet infinitis periculis immersus uideatur mortem appetere,tamen uiuere multò magis quã mori eligere.

ΑΝΥΣ

Ἐπιμύϑιον.

Ὁ μῦϑΘ ∆ηλοῖ,ὅτι πᾶς ἄνϑρωπΘ φιλό ζωΘ ὢν , κᾂν μυρίοις κινδύνοις ωⱦριπεσὼν ∂ονῇ θανάτε ἐπιϑυμᾷν· ὅμως τὸ ζῆν πολὺ ωⱦὸ τοῦ θανάτου αἱρᾶται.

Γραῦς

mental, and emphasised in typographical layout and choice of fount. 'Emblematic' fables too started from the illustration (originally on the left-hand page) which with its '*inscriptio*' and '*subscriptio*' occupied a whole side and was faced by the fable – usually in rhyme – as commentary. The fable was followed by moral reinforcements taken from history, classical antiquity or the Bible (see also pp. 46, 48, 68).

Both fable and emblem rely on a combination of word and picture, and both communicate accepted truths. An emblem cannot exist without its illustration: the image comes first. A fable however can fulfil its purpose without any emblematic device, since the text can stand by itself. Fables were told long before they were written down and given pictures: the words always came first.

6. THE CORMORANT, THE BRAMBLE AND THE BAT

It once happened that three partners – the cormorant trading in brass pots, the bramble in clothes, and the bat (that creature which is classed between the mice and the birds) borrowing money with interest to finance his ventures – loaded a ship with their goods. They set sail confidently, the hope of gain blinding them to peril – when suddenly a raging storm attacked the wretched creatures and with its impetuous whirlwinds destroyed at once the ship and their profits. Wet and helpless, they barely escaped the waves. Since that time, the cormorant frequents the foaming shore in case the waves, as they dash on the beach, should restore to him his brass vessels from the sea, and the bramble frequents the fields, catching with his rough barbs at all the clothes he meets in case he should by chance find his own. But the bat, who has long owed a sum of money (the interest now increased by the passage of time), *fearing to be dunned by daylight roams secretly by night.

*Debtors were immune from prosecution before sunrise.

Our frailties return to plague us, and the tide of bad habit carries us off against our will.

A. S. H.

Fabulae centum ex antiquis auctoribus delectae et a Gabriele Faerno Cremonensi carminibus explicatae. [Edited posthumously by Silvio Antoniano. Engraved by Pirro Ligorio.] 4to. Romae, Vincentius Luchinus (1563) 2.v.1868

At the request of his uncle and patron Pope Pius IV, the poet Faerno collected together his apologues based on Avianus and Phaedrus, but died before their first printing. Faerno took as his pattern Laurentius Abstemius' *Hecatomythion* (Venice, 1495): Latin verses rounded off with an epigrammatic moral. In spite of their wide circulation and renown outside Italy – the fables were first published in London in 1564 – Perrault's version of 1699 was almost the earliest translation into a vernacular. The illustrations, entirely new in composition and iconography, came to be attributed in the eighteenth century to the Bolognese Bartolomeo Passarotti, but the artist has now been established as Faerno's friend Pirro Ligorio. Ligorio was unusual for his time in combining a draughtsman's skill with the knowledge of an antiquary. His collection of drawings of Roman statuary led him to imagine the fable-gods as statues, and influenced his treatment of drapery. For the first time an attempt was made to show cause and effect as well as action, and to include each stage of the action rather than a single episode.

No other Italian series was imitated in Northern Europe, and these designs reappear with slight alterations in several Italian editions; they inspired the handsome full-page woodcuts by Titian's pupil Verdizotti for his own hundred verse fables of 1570. Titian may indeed have been involved to some degree. The Faerno pictures were apparently unknown to Gheeraerts and his motifs play little part in the principal line of descent – from mediaeval Germany via Gheeraerts to Bewick's England. Ligorio was probably the first fable-illustrator to discover the advantages of etching, a process uniquely suited to the demands of animal illustration and which Gheeraerts and his successors were soon and so effectively to exploit.

MERGVS, RVBVS, VESPERTILIO.

7. OF THE LION AND THE RAT

A Lion who once did a Rat some favour, prompted by his noble nature, falls into a net where for all his cunning he cannot help himself, however hard he struggles. Here he is, this poor Lion, caught in these bonds and ever raging, becoming yet more entangled as he roars. He uses both his strength and his skill to free himself, but all to no avail. The Rat, hearing his cries, quickly runs to the trap. He gnaws at the threads, and the Lion escapes. Then he promises to grant the Rat whatsoever favour he might desire, at any time and at any place.

Sometimes even the weak and insignificant may well find themselves in a position to repay the great and powerful for a kindness received.

Every man can make recompense.
  *Eccl.*12. v.1, 2
  1. When thou wilt do good, know to whom thou doest it; so shalt thou be thanked for thy benefits.
  2. Do good to the godly man, and thou shalt find a recompence.

A.S.H.

Esbatement moral, des animaux. [By Pierre Heyns. Engraved mainly after Marcus Gheeraerts.] 4to. A Anvers, chez Philippe Galle (chez Gerard Smits), 1578.   6.x.1863

The outstanding fable illustrations of the sixteenth century were designed by Marcus Gheeraerts the Elder of Bruges for Edewaerd de Dene's *De Warachtighe Fabulen der Dieren* (de Clerck, 1567, dedicated by Gheeraerts to the artist, numismatist and savant Hubert Goltzius), an adaptation for the most part of the earliest 'emblematic' fable-book – by the French poet Corrozet, printed in Paris by Janot in 1542 (see p. 26). De Dene was a member of the 'Rederijker' or Rhetoricians, a writers' guild which introduced emblem art into the Netherlands and was associated with the Dutch struggle for freedom. His fable-collection was one of the Calvinist books which – since the text was kept general – escaped censorship by the Spanish Inquisition.

The *Esbatement moral* was a French verse adaptation of de Dene in the form of sonnets by the poet Pierre Heyns (?) and an unspecified 'E. W.'. The plates (with the exception of eighteen new etched designs by Gheeraerts) were executed by an unknown engraver, perhaps Galle himself or Pieter Huys, a pupil of Brueghel the Elder. Gheeraerts' pictures had an unforeseen success and a long and complicated inheritance. The more distinguished editions containing them were usually emblematic in format, a Biblical quotation in metre replacing the emblem – as was the *Esbatement*, though related by its title to the mediaeval 'Bauernposse', a kind of farce. Its title page, showing Aesop on stage (see also p. 123), relates it to the world of theatre; a later version was actually called *Théâtre des animaux*.

Gheeraerts was one of the foremost animal painters of the day, his designs serving as aids for goldsmiths and other artists. He drew from life as far as possible, much indebted to zoological reproductions of Conrad Gesner's *Historia animalium* (1551–58). Depending chiefly on French and German models – Salomon, Solis, the *Ulm Aesop* (pp. 35, 43, 53) – he borrowed too from Alciati's emblems (through

Salomon) and was influenced by the painting and engraving of Pieter Brueghel and his circle, to which his Low Countries landscapes bear witness. Roman ruins appear here and there as a gesture to contemporary enthusiasm for Renaissance Italy: Gheeraerts' landscapes are seldom invented. He broke away from the woodcut, a technique which had till then dominated fable illustration. Etching, 'by substituting one freely moving scratch of a needle for two stiff cuts of a knife' (Hodnett 1979), was much better adapted to suggesting the feel of fur and feathers and the presence of a living creature.

'Even more than Salomon and Solis, Gheeraerts made the Aesopic event always seem part of an enveloping scene continuously receding into the distance.' With its wealth of precise detail and increased activity in middle distance and background, Gheeraerts' Aesop series stands at the head of a new tradition in European book illustration: a faithful realism which remained unchallenged till the eighteenth century.

8. OF THE HORSE, AND THE ASS LADEN WITH WOOD

No man should be too proud of his good fortune
Nor consider work to be a misfortune.

The Ass who day and night was tormented by toil and meagrely rewarded for it, meeting a fine Horse, well fed and unburdened, considered himself unlucky in having to bear so many blows with no respite. The Horse led such a pleasant life, but he, the Ass, had to be content with his calling, however wearisome he found it. He continued as usual with his work, but how reluctantly and how much more sluggishly, because he saw the Horse being pampered while he had to wear himself out fetching wood. It so happened that the Horse suffered the unexpected and was saddled and bridled to go to war. When the Ass saw this he went happily on his way and exerted himself in his misfortune, for fear of worse things.

MORAL ALLUSION

Fortune was never constant and favourable to anyone without eventually bringing him troubles. It often happens that the man who lives in comfort is overtaken by adversity and that his luck changes. Thinking himself secure, a bitter sorrow soon comes upon him, just as if he were a poor martyred slave – and in this state he dies. Let no one despair of his fortune, whether good or ill.

I *Cor.*10, v.12   Wherefore let him that thinketh he standeth take heed lest he fall *through his ambition, for he who amuses himself in the days of his good fortune may wantonly stumble into misfortune, unprotected by God.*

A. S. H.

XXV. fables des animaux. Vray miroir exemplaire, par lequel toute personne raisonnable pourra voir & comprendre, avec plaisir & contentement d'esprit, la conformité & vraye similitude de la personne ignorante ... aux animaux & bestes brutes. Composé et mis en lumiere par Estienne Perret, citoyen d'Anvers. [Engraved after Marcus Gheeraerts.] Fol. A Anvers, par Christophle Plantin, pour l'Aucteur, 1578.   22.vi.1869

Perret's fables, printed in the same year and city as the *Esbatement moral* (pp. 46-7), were again illustrated with Gheeraerts' designs. The engraver, one of Gheeraerts' first and least slavish followers, may have been Pieter Huys, but several engravings in the 1617 edition are signed by the Haarlem master Jan van de Velde II. The size alone of the plates, more than double that of their predecessors and larger than any to date in a fable-book, makes this one of the most imposing collections of its time. The additions and elaborations occur mainly on the upper half of the plate, and the original proportions have been lost; also, since the compositions are reversed the picture can no longer be 'read' from left to right.

This flat but conscientious rendering of twenty-four fables selected from de Dene's one hundred and seven was paid for by its author, the politician and poet Steven Perret. The edition was known to La Fontaine, who clearly took Perret's verses as a model, even helping himself to actual words or constructions. It is the most representative fable-book in emblematic form of the Gheeraerts succession.

9. THE CRAB AND THE FOX

A Restless *Crab*, in th'Ocean bred,
Stroll'd out, and in a Meadow fed;
But by a *Fox* was soon espy'd,
Soon made his Prey, and justly dy'd:
For had he stay'd at home contented,
All had been well, his Fate prevented.
    Thus restless Fools, who Business quit,
And aim at Marks they ne'er can hit,
The Smart of sure Miscarriage bear,
For rambling in a foreign Sphere.

APPLICATION

A Rolling Stone gathers no Moss.

Some People are so possessed with the Spirit of Rambling, and, as they foolishly call it, trying their Fortune, that though they have all the Conveniencies of Life at Home, yet they can't be contented, but must sally out into the wide World at all Adventures. A severe Repentance however, after such Elopements, is for the most Part as certain, as it is altogether useless and unregarded.

Select Tales and Fables [by B. Cole?], before 1746

Centum fabulae ex antiquis scriptoribus acceptae, et graecis, latinisq́; tetrastichis senariis explicatae à Fabio Paulino Utinensi. [Woodcuts mainly after Bernard Salomon.] 12mo. Venetiis, apud Haeredes Francisci Ziletti, 1587.   697-1887

The picture which so plausibly accompanies this fable is an example of the repetition or wrong ordering of designs which often occurred in the late sixteenth century. For Cesare Pavesi's collection of twenty years earlier, it had illustrated 'The Dog and the Meat' (reproduced on p. 57 in a version by Hollar).

Salomon's Lyons designs, much copied in France and Italy (see pp. 42–3), were still in circulation a hundred years later, as were these woodcuts – used not only for Pavesi and Paulinus but for Giulio Landi's popular four-hundred-fable compendium of 1575, again printed in Venice. The eye is drawn by the angle of the dog's body to the backdrop of bridge and town in the middle distance, serenely indifferent to the dramatic moment. Such localised settings are a distinguishing mark of the unknown artist who created this perfectly balanced little cameo.

Paulinus' bilingual adaptation with Greek and Latin parallel text was of a type general at the time and favoured by schools.

Ο γ΄.

Καρκῖνος, καὶ ἀλώπηξ.

Θαλάσσης ἐξιὼν ἀλᾶτ᾽ ἀντίω νέμων
Καρκῖνος, ἥδε κερδώ ἥρπασ᾽ ὡς φάγοι,
Ὁ δ᾽ αὖ ἔφη, θνήξων, μοι ἀξίως τάδ᾽, ὃς
Χερσαῖος. ἤθελον εἶναι, ὢν θαλάσσιος.

Επιμύθιον. (πει.

Προλιποῦσ᾽ ἑὰς τέχνας κακὸν καλῶς πρέ

LXXIII.

Cancer, & Vulpes.

Cancer mari egressus vagabatur foris
Pascens, fame Vulpes furens rapit, vt edat.
Hic deuorandus iam iam, ait, merito hac mihi,
Qui animans maris cū sim, esse terrestre volui.

Sensus fab.

Artes suas qui deserunt, mala hos decent.

D 5   PISCA-

10. A FOX AND A GOAT

A *Fox* and a *Goat* went down by consent into a Well to Drink, and when they had Quench'd their Thirst, the *Goat* fell to Hunting up and down which way to get back again. Oh! says *Reynard*, Never trouble your Head how to get back, but leave That to me. Do but you raise your self upon your hinder-Legs with your fore-Feet close to the Wall, and then stretch out your Head; I can easily whip up to your Horns, and so out of the Well, and draw you after me. The *Goat* puts himself in a Posture immediately, as he was directed, gives the *Fox* a Lift, and so out he springs; but *Reynard*'s Business was now only to make Sport with his Companion, instead of Helping him. Some hard Words the *Goat* gave him, but the *Fox* puts off all with a Jest. If you had but half so much Brain as Beard, says he, you would have bethought your self how to get up again before you went down.

THE MORAL

A Wise Man will Debate every Thing Pro *and* Con *before he comes to Fix upon any Resolution. He leaves Nothing to Chance more than needs must. There must be no Bant'ring out of Season.*

L'Estrange, 6 edn, 1714

Fabulae Aesopi graecè & latinè, nunc denuo selectae: eae item quas Avienus carmine expressit. [New edition. Engraved on wood by Christoffel van Sichem after Vergil Solis.] 8vo. Amsterodami, apud Joannem Janssonium, 1653.   962–1887

A long series of scholastic fable editions was printed in the sixteenth century, beginning with Martin Dorp's five hundred fables of 1513 and continued in the Dutch collection edited by Daniel Heinsius (officially commissioned as a textbook from 1626). For convenience – and because of the contradictory nature of the morals? – they normally contained only selected fables with simple Latin texts for translation or stylistic exercises, and were printed in pocket-book form.

   Christoffel van Sichem's cuts, which first appeared in the 1626 edition, derive from the series by Vergil Solis, first printed in Frankfurt in 1566 and bringing the Italianate influence of Janot and Salomon to Germany. Both Salomon and Solis used the traditional woodcut method and, though Solis was not primarily a book artist, both illustrated the Bible, Ovid and Aesop: the *Aesop* was done shortly before Solis' death. All but a few of the designs were reproductions, about three-quarters being taken from Salomon's Lyons cuts (see p. 43) and a quarter from Zainer's *Ulm Aesop* of a century earlier. Since Solis employed larger blocks than Salomon the cutting could be stronger and clearer, giving a perhaps undeserved effect of originality and vivacity of detail. Neither Salomon nor Solis contrive to make their animals individually striking, or more than part of a generally lively and appealing scene.

11. THE SUN AND THE WIND

There happen'd a Controversy betwixt the *Sun* and the *Wind*, which was the Stronger of the Two; and they put the Point upon this Issue: There was a Traveller upon the Way, and which of the Two could make that Fellow Quit his Cloak should carry the Cause. The *Wind* fell presently a Storming and threw Hail-shot over and above in the very Teeth of him. The Man wraps himself up, and keeps Advancing still in spight of the Weather: But this Gust in a short Time blew over: And then the *Sun* brake out, and fell to Work upon him with his Beams; but still he Pushes forward, Sweating, and Panting, till in the End he was forc'd to Quit his Cloak, and lay himself down upon the Ground in a Cool Shade for his Relief: So that the *Sun*, in the Conclusion, carry'd the Point.

THE MORAL

Reason and Resolution will Support a Man against all the Violences of Malice and Fortune; but in a Wallowing Qualm, a Man's Heart and Resolution fails him, for want of Fit Matter to Work upon.

REFLECTION

'Tis a Part of good Discretion in all Contests, to Consider over and over, the Power, the Strength, and the Interest of our Adversary: and likewise again, that though One Man may be more Robust than Another, that Force may be Baffled yet by Skill and Address. It is in the Bus'ness of Life as it is in a Storm, or a Calm Sea: The Blast may be Impetuous; but seldom last long; and though the Vessel be Press'd never so hard, a Skilful Steers-man will yet bear up against it: But in a Dead-Calm, a Man loses his Spirits, and lies in a Manner Expos'd, as the Scorn and Spectacle of Ill Fortune.

L'Estrange, 6 edn, 1714

The Fables of Aesop Paraphras'd in Verse, and Adorn'd with Sculpture, by John Ogilby. [Engraved by Franz Cleyn.] 4to. London, by Thomas Warren, for Andrew Crook, 1651. 2.xii.1870

At the age of forty the Royalist poet, printer, actor, dancing-master and cosmographer John Ogilby began to learn Latin, and to translate Aesop into English verse. He brought out four *Aesops* of which three, achieved almost entirely by two artists, are masterpieces of seventeenth-century book illustration. Ogilby's quarto *Aesop Paraphras'd* of 1651 was the first English fable-book of any consequence since Caxton, and his free adaptation, though derided by Dryden and Pope, anticipates their epic style. Ogilby, who also made powerful translations of Virgil and Homer, tried to improve on existing texts and give them narrative continuity. His was the first 'polite' edition (see pp. 19, 21), addressed to children as well as to adults: many writers insisted that their fables, though thoroughly sophisticated in language and worldly in content, were intended for young readers. Till then no English fable-writer had dared to express so overtly Royalist resentment of the political situation under Cromwell.

Ogilby's *Aesop* was assigned to the painter and tapestry-designer Franz Cleyn, who in 1625 had been invited from Denmark by James I to head the Royal tapestry

65

works at Mortlake. Cleyn was the earliest known illustrator of real importance in England after Gheeraerts, if judged by the quantity rather than the quality of his work, which was however still inferior to the Continental product. In imitation of Gheeraerts, Cleyn both drew and etched his plates. The series is significant as a link between the Continent and England – between Gheeraerts and Hollar, Cleyn's more illustrious successor.

In the past designs for illustration had been treated as common property. Cleyn was more concerned than most about his borrowings, which he camouflaged with care and cunning – but a certain originality in the introduction of new items reveals an unusual familiarity with the fables. Though his compositions are sometimes cluttered, with elements haphazardly and gracelessly arranged and with irrelevant and weakly bitten figures in the background, Cleyn always remains true to the text.

12. OF THE DOG AND SHADOW

This Dog away with a whole Shoulder ran,
Let thanks be to the careless Larder-Man,
Which made the Proverb true: both large and good
The Mutton was, no way but take the Flood;
His fellow-Spaniels waiting in the Hall,
Nay Hounds, and Currs, in for a share would fall;
Those Beggars, that like Plague and Famine sit
Guarding the Gate, would eat both him and it;
Shrewd were his doubts lest Serving-Men might put
In for their part, and strive for the first cut;
A thousand real Dangers thus persuade,
As many more his nimble fancy made;
Faces about, straight at a Postern-Gate
He takes the Stream, and leaves the rest to Fate.

   'Twas in the *Dog-daies* too, the Skies were cleer,
Not one black-patch did in Heaven's face appear:
Breathless the Sun left two and thirty Winds,
And such the Calm as that the *Halcyon* finds.

   When a refracted Ray, a golden Beam
In the gross *Medium* of the darker Stream
Pencil'd an other Shoulder like to that
The Dog had purchas'd, but more large, and fat.
To him who oft had fed from Beggars Caps,
Shar'd in the Dole, and quarrell'd for faln Scraps,
With twenty more for a gnawn bone would fight,
A greedy Worm, a dogged Appetite
Gave sad advice, to seize one Shoulder more.
(*Some Mortals till they'r Rich are never Poor.*)
Too rash he bites: down to the deepest Stream
The Shadow and the Substance, like a Dream

Vanish'd together; thrice he dives in vain;
For the swift Current bore it to the Main,
To furnish *Triton*'s Banquet, who that day
Married the famous Mermaid *Galate*.
The Virgin smil'd, but yet the easie Nymph
Return'd not, for the Present, one poor Shrimp.

   Thrice round he looks, raising his woful head,
To see which way the Feather'd Joynt was fled;
But finding none, he is resolv'd to die,
And with his Love dear Lady Mutton lie.
Yet hating a wet Death, he swam to shore,
Then set a Throat up made the Welking rore;
To hang himself in his own collar he
Is next resolv'd, could he but find a Tree.
Full of despair, there down himself he flung
Then thus his howling Recantation sung;

   Here I the Emblem of fond Mortals sit,
That lose the substance for an Empty bit:
Whom fair pretences, and a hollow shade
Of future Happiness, Unhappy made:
Nay States, and mighty Realms, with plenty proud,
Thus for Rich *Juno* oft imbrace a Cloud.
He is too blest that his own happiness knows,
And Mortals to themselves are greatest Foes.

MORAL

Foul Avarice is of pregnant Mony bred;
He that loves Gold, starves more, the more he's fed:
Doubling of thousands Usurers to their cost
Know, when both Use and Principall is lost.

The Fables of Aesop Paraphras'd in Verse: Adorn'd with Sculpture, and Illustrated with Annotations. By John Ogilby, Esq. [New edition. Engraved by Wenzel Hollar and Dirk Stoop.] Fol. London, by Thomas Roycroft, for the Author, 1665. Clements Bequest L.2320–1948

The larger designs needed for this reprint of Ogilby's 1651 *Aesop* were nearly all conceived by Wenzel Hollar (see p. 27). Ogilby had 'paraphrased' the fables in verse but Hollar managed nothing so imaginative: his motifs came from Cleyn, and Gheeraerts inspired his method. The problem of how best to represent the dog's reflection relative to the position of the sun has resulted in an interesting assortment of illustrative solutions to this ancient fable. Its interpretation, just as complex, has swung between the sacred and the profane in accordance with the prevailing moral climate. On a purely practical level, it is a reminder that thieving will be punished and that we should be content with what we have; the spiritual lesson is that in striving after worldly gain we are in danger of forfeiting eternal bliss.

the Dog and Shadow.

24

13. OF THE CRAB AND HER MOTHER

Had ever *Hielding Crabat* such a *Miene*?
Stil hobling side-ward, thy foul claws turn'd in!
Base Maggots in a Magnifying Glass
'Mongst Chedar Common-wealths more comly pace,
Conducting busie *Mites* from Grange to Grange,
Forts raising or to build their new Exchange.

How wouldst thou of Step-stately Ladies learn,
To raise a Dust, trailing thy Silken stern;
Couldst thou but get into the City Vain,
To trip up *Maiden*, or down *Mincing-Lane*;
I might be pleas'd with such a decent Sight,
Though Modesty be out of fashion quite.

Thus Beldam *Crab*, her *Crablin* Daughter chid,
Because she hirpl'd as her Mother did.

When thus her ill-pac'd Little one reply'd;
Still you lie Baiting, always Braul and Chide;
Examples are best Precepts, Talk's but talk,
Leave finding fault, and shew me how to Walk.

The Mother then; Daughter y' are very short,
Though Blows more fit than Words are, to retort;
I'll take advice; Come! bridle close your Chin,
Thrust out your Breast, and keep your Belly in.

When I was Young, and little as thou art,
I led a *Bevie* fir'd by *Cupid*'s Dart,
From Mountain Seats to pay accustom'd Scores
In *Thetis* Watery Court to brisk Amours;
With steady and Majestick pace we walk'd,
Nor Precipices, Rocks, nor Rivers baulk'd,
Ne'r deviating step, till in the Main,
Brisk Males attending us did entertain.

Come, follow me, I once did learn to Dance;
Walk'd stately measures that ne'r came from *France*;
The *Fairy* Court admir'd me, and Queen *Mab*
Grew Jealous, though grown now a wither'd *Crab*;
So! to the Right, nor to the Left hand swerve,
But me your Mother, punctually observe.

Th'old Beldam thus, Hipshotten and Bunch back,
Deni'd by Nature, Amble, Trot, or Rack,
Her Daughter taught, to whom at last she said;
You tread awry, and I move Retrograde:
My steps like yours, as Coyn drops from the Mint,
With like Impressions yielding sand imprint:
But if my Observations be true,
Court Madams waddle now like me or you;
Who should Exemplars be, give others Rules,
Waving Formalities of Boarding-Schools,
Taking proud freedoms scorn restraintive Law,
Like Ships in Storms at Anchor rowl and Yaw,
No more 'gainst me and my Behaviour preach,
First learn your self, and then your Daughter teach;
Who best are stor'd with Ignorance and Pride,
Most others Imbecillities Deride.

MORAL

Age, Youth Instructs, Vices whate'r to shun,
Whilst Children o'r their Parents Footsteps run:
Mothers their Daughters in the Oven find
Where once They hid; and Cat will after Kind.

Aesopic's: or a Second Collection of Fables, Paraphras'd in Verse: Adorn'd with Sculpture, and Illustrated with Annotations. By John Ogilby, Esq. [Engraved by Hollar and others.] Fol. London, by Thomas Roycroft, for the Author, 1668.   Clements Bequest   L.2321-1948

To recover the losses made on his *Aesop Paraphras'd* of 1665, destroyed in the Great Fire of London, Ogilby planned a second collection with another fifty fables for which he commissioned thirty-six designs from the itinerant Bohemian artist Hollar, and Stoop. Being overworked and underpaid, Hollar not surprisingly depended on pre-existing models and proffered no completely new insight into the texts. He made use of Barlow's recently printed folio *Aesop* (see pp. 62-3) and even asked Barlow to share in the work. The King sent Hollar to Tangier before the job could be completed, so that half the illustrations had to be left to Barlow and others; the results were uneven in quality.

The *Aesopics* did not live up to the reputation of the 1665 collection in spite of some exceptionally fine plates - notably 'The Two Crabs', a design far more fresh

and striking than previous handlings of the subject. The early woodcuts had merely shown two monstrous shellfish on a bank, and even Gheeraerts' crayfish swimming in the river lack the charm of Hollar's crabs etched in arresting and detailed close-up, their claws entwined (Hodnett 1979).

14. THE FOX AND CRANE

The Fox provides a Feast, invites a Crane,
Who soon accepts to show him no disdain:
The Dish was flat, so liquid was the meat,
That th'Crane must fast, Reynard alone must eat.

Upon a Rock stands a Fox with a Crane.
The Fox holding his snout on a flat gilded Dish;
The water spreads it self in form of a Table Cloth,
The Crane spouts up water into the Air.

Description

THE CRANE AND FOX

This mutual Love was soon return'd again,
Reynard's invited by his Friend the Crane.
The Meat's brought in a Jug, the Mouth's so strait,
Poor Reynard must go home to lick his Plate.

English version by J. Morisson, 1677

Labyrinte de Versailles. [Thirty-nine fables of Aesop in quatrains by Isaac de Benserade, the original prose descriptions by Charles Perrault. New edition. Engraved by Sébastien Le Clerc.] 4to. t'Amsteldam, by Nicolaus Visscher [1682?] 13.vi.1870

One of Le Nôtre's most ingenious creations was the maze at Versailles, where thirty-nine animal fountains in painted lead were set at the intersections of the *allées* so that from each crossing-point several fountains could be seen. The fountains were representations of fables – this one shows half of a 'double fable' – positioned so as to emphasise their rôle as a guide through the maze, and through life itself. Each pedestal was incised with a fable quatrain by the Court Poet Isaac de Benserade, which so delighted Louis XIV that the poet was encouraged to compose further epigrams. They were included in Perrault's description of the maze, first published in Paris in 1677 and followed by variant editions, all with engravings by Sébastien Le Clerc, teacher of geometry, perspective and architecture at the Académie Royale and sometimes called inventor of the vignette. A translation by Daniel Bellamy senior was published in his son's *Ethic Amusements* (London, 1768) with engravings by George Bickham.

Fashions in garden architecture changed, and in 1775 the fountains were destroyed apart from a few pieces of sculpture. Le Clerc's designs remain the only record of these rare three-dimensional renderings of the fables.

De Vos en de Kraan vogel.

v. S. F. *By Nicolaus Visscher met Privilegie.*

13

15. THE OX AND TOAD

The Toad woud needs the Oxes size attaine,
And with fell poyson puffs up every veine,

Then askd her sone if equall were their size,
Then swells againe, and with her venome dyes.

MORALL

*The woud-bee witts to Lawrrels woud aspire,
And write till damn'd they shamefully retire.*

Aphra Behn

Aesop's Fables with his Life: in English, French and Latin. Newly translated. Illustrated with ... sculptures ... by Francis Barlow. [New edition.] Fol. London, by H. Hills jun., for Francis Barlow, 1687.   29.ii.1868

The *Aesop* of Francis Barlow, the earliest native-born English book illustrator, is his best-known work: it was the most important English *Aesop* even in Bewick's day. The original edition had been printed in 1666, a year after Ogilby's folio collection, but most copies vanished in the Great Fire of London. Barlow's one hundred and ten vigorous compositions - which he etched himself - gave fresh impetus to the ever-persisting influence of Marcus Gheeraerts' genre pictures, which had yielded a whole succession of imitations since their first appearance in 1567. They culminated in this new and free interpretation, which developed the traditional motifs and was itself admired and emulated for many generations, travelling via Kirkall as far as Bewick's *Fables* of 1818 (see pp. 86-7). Barlow gleaned from nearly all the chief sources, some in late editions or copies, for instance Gesner's *Historia animalium.* Nearly half his designs - and his emphatic, linear manner - come from Gheeraerts (in a late edition) and an astonishing number from Cleyn, but about a quarter appear to be original conceptions.

Sporting themes were especially popular in the seventeenth century. Barlow, 'father of the British sporting print' (Hodnett 1979), was the first true animal specialist in this country. He approached his subjects in a spirit of scientific curiosity and, typically for the period, depicted each animal as itself and in its natural surroundings. The fable-creatures are realised with affection and treated with respect. No longer are they invested with symbolic meaning, nor are they humans in disguise - except that each is made to express as much as possible the mood or state demanded by the fable in which it performs: fear or anger, aggression or pride.

Even more than Gheeraerts, Barlow 'in turning fable illustrations from humorous pantomime or stylized morality plays into often moving domestic drama' (Hodnett 1979) achieved 'a sense of credibility that is the mark of distinguished illustration'.

The Toad woud needs the Oxes size attaine,   Then askd her sone if equall were their size,
And with fell poyson puffs up every veine,   Then swells againe, and with her penome dyes.

Morall

The woud-bee witts to Lawrels woud aspire,
And write till damn'd, they shamefully retire.

16. OF A CHAMELEON, AND A PARASITE

A Chameleon saw some people tormenting a parasite which had been annoying a great Lord, and was accused of resembling it. The chameleon, cut to the quick by the comparison, could not refrain from saying that the parallel which they drew between him and this glutton was quite unjust, since *he* lived on air alone and his metamorphoses troubled no one, whereas this Parasite was a burden on everyone and never paid his way – unless with base and shameful flatteries.

MORAL

Parasites and swindlers are a plague, and obnoxious to all.

A. S. H.

Fables d'Esope, avec les figures de Sadeler [engraved after Gheeraerts]. Traduction nouvelle. 8vo. A Paris, chez Pierre Aubouyn, Pierre Emery & Charles Clouzier (de Laurent Rondet), 1689.   15.ix.1877

The accurate reproduction of etchings calls for exceptional skill, and Sadeler's art was equal to the task. Some of the best Gheeraerts copies are to be found in his collection of German verse fables: the still emblematic *Theatrum morum* (Prague, 1608), much in vogue in Bohemia. Sadeler, summoned by the Emperor Rudolph, took the Gheeraerts pictures with him to Prague and added fifteen items of his own; their accomplishment and sophistication harmonise perfectly with the Gheeraerts series. These same plates are used in the 1659, 1689 and 1743 French versions, edited and provided with prose commentaries by the celebrated numismatist and bibliophile Raphaël Trichet du Fresne, and undoubtedly seen by La Fontaine.

'No matter how extraordinary the main action, it seems credible because life goes tranquilly on immediately behind it' (Hodnett 1979). The surprising spectacle of a chameleon from Gesner on a Flemish river bank strikes no discordant note because of Gheeraerts' gift for mixing the unfamiliar with the everyday. Besides, such paradoxes were part of the emblem tradition. Gheeraerts' refined engraving technique allowed a depth of perspective and a degree of background detail till then unknown, but the significance of the fables on an allegorical level brings us back from the particular to the general.

17. THE SATYR AND THE PEASANT

A *Countryman* found lost in the wood a shaggy *Satyr* who, well-nigh dead with cold, sat cowering in a hollow. He brought him into his house and made him welcome. The *Satyr*, man above but beast below, observed that the *Peasant* blew into his fists to protect his hands and warm his knuckles, almost numb with the cold of the windy fields. He saw too that when the victuals were put on the table-top, the *Peasant* blew away the burning heat with his breath. Amazed at this, he took fright and fled from the house in fear of his life because the man could blow hot and cold with the same breath.

A wise man takes care to avoid those who can hold fire in one hand and water in the other, for although they appear kind and benevolent, they are not without wicked wiles.

Emanuel the Greek Emperor in a certain affair showed himself to be both hot and cold, both friend and foe. For when the Emperor *Conradus* advanced with his army into Palestine, Emanuel affected to be very helpful and obliging, supplying him with grain and all kinds of provisions. But he had lime mixed with the grain, so that the fighting-men became grievously ill and suffered heavy losses. Now when *Conradus* perceived this, to wit that *Emanuel* was friendly in word and hostile in deed, trusting him no longer he promptly made good his escape. (SABELLICUS)

A. S. H.

Vorstelijcke Warande der Dieren: ... met Exempelen uyt de Oude Historien, in Prose; ende Uytleggingen, in Rijm verklaert, door J[oost] v[an den] V[ondel]. Verciert met [125] afbeeldingen, in koper gesneden, door Marcus Gerards. [First published in 1617 by Dierck Pietersz Pers. 5th edition?] 4to. t'Amsterdam, by d'Erve de Wed: Gysbert de Groot [c. 1725?] 14.v.1868

Inferior copies of the sixteenth-century plates appear as late as 1786, in the last-known edition of this Netherlandish adaptation of Heyns' *Esbatement moral* (pp. 46–7) by the eminent poet and dramatist Joost van den Vondel. The '*Princely Menagerie*' was another of the 'emblematic' fable-books, with the tripartite structure of motto, picture and moral, and a commentary in the form of a verse fable. The first editor added captions from the Bible, Church fathers and authors of antiquity, or (as here) from history: Sabellico was a Venetian historian.

Success and sustained popularity were ensured for van den Vondel's work by his adoption of Gheeraerts' pictures with their realistic anatomy and milieu and their vivid portrayal of emotion, whether of men or of beasts. His satyr's expression of mistrust is quite unmistakeable. The homely genre setting is typical: Hodnett (1979) observes that Gheeraerts 'had a modest but definite rôle in shifting taste in book illustration from aristocratic remoteness to democratic involvement in the immediate scene'.

18. OF THE JAY ADORNED WITH PEACOCK'S FEATHERS

A Jay who wanted to play the beau adorned himself with all the Peacock's feathers he could gather. He was so proud of this borrowed ornament that he scarcely deigned to look at other birds. He had been vain enough however to introduce himself among the Peacocks, who having discovered his trickery set about tearing out his feathers, the first plucking out one feather and the next another till at last he was reduced to his original state.

———— ;❧ ————

MORAL REFLECTIONS

This fable illustrates very well the extravagant ambition of those people who want to follow the fashion and mingle rashly with persons of distinction, thinking to dazzle by their artifices. Such foolish vanity is rather to be laughed at than condemned, because the natural instinct of a ·Peasant cannot be changed by his costume: a Jay will always remain a Jay even if adorned fifty times over with Peacock's feathers, just as a Peasant is still a Peasant even if clothed in princely garments. How many people one sees these days who, driven by blind presumption, have the effrontery to impose themselves on people of quality, unwilling to acknowledge the differences bestowed by breeding and nurture. These arrogant creatures deck themselves out in a superb wardrobe; they borrow the plumage of the great, run up debts on all sides, and provoke nothing but mirth with their affectations and borrowed mannerisms. But being in no position to continue living in this style, they are besieged by their creditors, each demanding his portion - and in the end these make-believe Gentlemen are lucky if the bailiffs don't mistake them for the servants.

*Eccl.*11, v.4 Boast not of thy clothing and raiment...
The habit does not make the monk, but rather the rules and customs he observes. It is an affectation betraying pride, not humility, to put on more than is necessary to cover one's body against the ravages of the elements. As a general reflection, it is evident that man has nothing of his own in which to clothe himself and that he flaunts what doesn't belong to him. If the sheep were to come and reclaim their wool, the earth its linen, the worms their silk, the mountains their gold and silver, oysters their pearls, and all the rest, what sort of fine figure could man cut in Society? Indeed, as Solon observed to Croesus, Cocks, Peacocks and Pheasants are happier than we are because their clothing is natural while ours is borrowed.

*Revel.*16, v.15 Blessed is he that watcheth, and keepeth his garments, lest he walk naked, and they see his shame.

A. S. H. (slightly adapted and abridged)

Trésor de fables, choisies des plus excellens mythologistes, accompagnées du sens moral, expliqué par l'Écriture Sainte. Avec des reflexions, des maximes, des proverbes & des exemples; tirés de l'histoire sacrée & profane. Orné ... par J. L. Krafft, graveur [mainly after Gheeraerts]. 4to. A Bruxelles, chés la Veuve G. Jacobs; (A Gand: chez la Veuve de Pierre de Goesin) 1734. 696-7-1886

In spite of innovations in fable illustration after 1700, the Gheeraerts designs continued to be re-used in various countries and in a variety of editions - yet even in

compositions as thoroughly indebted to their predecessors as these virtual facsimiles from van den Vondel (pp. 66-7), engraved mainly in reverse, the new arrangements suggest some attempt at inventiveness. Krafft's enjoyment of marine landscapes and full-rigged ships with billowing sails reveals itself in several plates where the background dominates the story – but this particular design is all discipline, its bird-actors framed by the clipped hedges of a formal garden. In comparison, Gheeraerts' originals teem with billowing peacock's tails, in one corner a mere glimpse of architecture.

By the early seventeenth century, fable-texts were more often in prose and less obviously emblematic in structure. This more recent version preserves the old discursive and didactic character, liberally peppered as was traditional with Biblical or historical allusions.

19. THE MAN, THE CAT, THE DOG, AND THE FLY

. . . In every rank, or great or small,
'Tis industry supports us all.

. . . The animals, by want opprest,
To Man their services addrest:
While each pursu'd their selfish good,
They hunger'd for precarious food;
Their hours with anxious cares were vext,
One day they fed, and starv'd the next:
They saw that plenty, sure and rife,
Was found alone in social life;
That, mutual industry profest
The various wants of Man redrest.

    The Cat, half-famish'd, lean and weak,
Demands the privilege to speak.

    Well, Puss, (says Man) and what can you
To benefit the public do?

    The Cat replies; These teeth, these claws,
With vigilance shall serve the cause.
The mouse, destroy'd by my pursuit,
No longer shall your feasts pollute;
Nor rats, from nightly ambuscade,
With wasteful teeth your stores invade.

    I grant, says Man, to gen'ral use
Your parts and talents may conduce;
For rats and mice purloin our grain,
And threshers whirl the flail in vain:
Thus shall the Cat, a foe to spoil,
Protect the farmer's honest toil.

    Then turning to the Dog, he cry'd,
Well, Sir; be next your merits try'd.

    Sir, says the Dog, by self-applause
We seem to own a friendless cause.
Ask those who know me, if distrust
E'er found me treach'rous or unjust.
Did I e'er faith, or friendship break?
Ask all those creatures; let them speak.
My vigilance and trusty zeal,
Perhaps might serve the public weal.
Might not your flocks in safety feed,
Were I to guard the fleecy breed?
Did I the nightly watches keep,
Could thieves invade you while you sleep?

    The Man replies, 'Tis just and right,
Rewards such service should requite.

So rare, in property, we find
Trust uncorrupt among mankind,
That, taken in a public view,
The first distinction is your due.
Such merits all reward transcend;
Be then my comrade and my friend.

    Addressing now the Fly. From you
What public service can accrue?

    From me! the flutt'ring insect said;
I thought you knew me better bred.
Sir, I'm a gentleman. Is't fit,
That I to industry submit?
Let mean mechanics, to be fed,
By bus'ness earn ignoble bread:
Lost in excess of daily joys,
No thought, no care, my life annoys.
At noon (the lady's matin hour)
I sip the tea's delicious flower:
On cates luxuriously I dine,
And drink the fragrance of the vine.
Studious of elegance and ease,
Myself alone I seek to please.

    The Man his pert conceit derides,
And thus the useless coxcomb chides.

    Hence, from that peach, that downy seat,
No idle fool deserves to eat.
Could you have sapp'd the blushing rind,
And on that pulp ambrosial din'd,
Had not some hand, with skill and toil,
To raise the tree, prepar'd the soil?
Consider, sot, what would ensue,
Were all such worthless things as you:
You'd soon be forc'd (by hunger stung)
To make your dirty meals on dung,
On which such despicable need,
Unpitied, is reduc'd to feed.
Besides, vain selfish insect, learn,
(If you can right and wrong discern)
That he who with industrious zeal,
Contributes to the public weal,
By adding to the common good,
His own hath rightly understood.

    So saying, with a sudden blow,
He laid the noxious vagrant low:
Crush'd in his luxury and pride,
The spunger on the public dy'd.

Fable VIII.

H. Gravelot, inv. et delin. Publish'd Sep. 29, 1738, by J. & P. Knapton, & T. Cox. G. Scotin Sculp.

Fables. By the late Mr Gay. Volume the second. The fifth edition. [Engraved by J.B.G. Scotin after H. Gravelot.] 8vo. London, for J. & P. Knapton, 1755. Townshend Bequest 9.x.1868

The affable and indolent John Gay – poet, playwright and friend of Swift and Pope – is most familiar to us as author of *The Beggar's Opera*. His modish verse fables, stylistically and dramatically derived from La Fontaine, owe little to folklore (see also p. 17). This fable is inscribed 'To my Native Country'.

The posthumous second volume (1738) was engraved by Scotin after Gravelot, pupil of Boucher and considered to be the first major practising book illustrator. It is diverting to compare this exercise in the play of light and shade – the diagonal lines of the sunbeam in harmonious contrast to the soft drapery folds and sinuous curves of chair-leg and cat – with Taylor's treatment for 'The Two Lamps' (p. 77) and with Agnes Miller Parker (p. 119).

20. A COCK AND A FOX

A Fox spying a Cock at roost in a tree with his Hens about him, wanted to get him down, and asked him, if he did not hear the news? What news, said the Cock? Why, replied the Fox, There's a general peace concluded among all living creatures, and not one of them is to presume, upon pain of life and limb, directly or indirectly to hurt another. The blessedest tidings in the world, says the Cock! and at the same time he stretches out his neck, as if he were looking at somewhat a great way off. What are you peering at? says the Fox. Nothing, says t'other, but a couple of great dogs yonder, that are coming this way, open-mouthed, as hard as they can drive. Why then, says Reynard, I fancy I'd e'en best be jogging. No, no says the Cock, the general peace will secure you: Ay, quoth the Fox, so it ought; but if these rascally curs should not have heard of the proclamation, I shall be but poorly off for all that. And so away he scampered.

MORAL

Perfidious people are naturally to be suspected in reports
that favour their own interest.

Samuel Richardson, 1740 [1739]

Fables choisies, mises en vers par J. de La Fontaine. [Engraved after C. N. Cochin's reworking of J. B. Oudry's designs, with woodcut ornaments after Bachelier by Papillon and Le Sueur.] Fol. A Paris, chez Desaint & Saillant, Durand, de l'Imprimerie de Charles-Antoine Jombert, 1755-59. 2432-5-1905

Favourite of the Queen and famous for his hunting tapestries, the painter Oudry 'scribbled in his spare hours' (1729-34) a cycle of designs to La Fontaine, taken from Chauveau or occasionally from the Gheeraerts tradition and intended for tapestries. The technique was too free for engraving - so Cochin redrew the designs, which a galaxy of engravers transferred to copper. Oudry never saw the finished work, now almost unrecognisable.

Already, sixty years after La Fontaine's death, the spirit of the age had changed and the underlying moral teaching of fables temporarily lost its significance. Oudry emphasises visual rather than conceptual aspects, with a stylised interpretation of the blander face of nature that matches the poet's superficial polish rather than his deeper meaning. The fables become picturesque anecdotes, set in civilised park scenery fit for the artificiality of a Fragonard pastoral. The universe has been transformed into spectacle (Riese-Hubert 1967) - even this static, conversational fable might be a scene from opera. As in classical theatre, the accustomed order is not disturbed and violence is kept in the wings, but here decor is all-important, with actors and objects pleasingly disposed in opulent interiors or idealised land-scapes. The sense of illusion is increased by architectural frames, each bearing the title as if on a plinth. Often this exuberance can distract attention from the plot, but the smooth and supple animals are modelled with a consciousness of tactile qualities, scrupulously observed and anatomically correct.

LE COQ ET LE RENARD. Fable XXXVII.

21. THE BEAR AND THE HONEY-BEES

A fastidious Bear, finicky and particular in his tastes (his Nurse had spoilt him), longed one day through a natural but ridiculous instinct to eat some honey – the dish had tempted him. The hives were nearby among the thyme and lavender: the thoughtless great creature, heeding nothing in his frenzied greed and made bold by anticipation, bounded forward and overturned them. The hives lay scattered all around him, and our Bear was quite delighted. But hardly had his enjoyment begun when the whole swarm fell upon him, stinging his eyes, his neck, his ears, his muzzle and clinging to the most sensitive places. Then, reinforced by a new swarm they pierced the rash beast with their invisible darts, buzzing all the while.

Let us learn from this Bear to rule our desires: the counsels of instinct are sometimes harmful, and pleasure often gives birth to pain.

A. S. H.

Fables nouvelles. (Fables par Mr. Dorat.) [Engraved after Clément Pierre Marillier. Volume I.] 8vo. A La Haye, Paris, chez Delalain, 1773.   4.xii.1874

The success of Dorat's trial fable-collection of 1772 encouraged him to follow it a year later with an expanded edition of one hundred fables; the second volume was delayed. Dorat was much concerned with the appearance of his poems and the staging of his plays, his defence being that naïve souls are swayed by pictures rather than ideas. More than twenty-five engravers were engaged in decorating the fables with headpieces and little tailpieces of considerable grace and charm, after the eminent vignettist Clément Pierre Marillier. They are set in classical imitation picture-frames, independently attractive and of various patterns. At the time this was a customary method of differentiating book illustrations from prints: here the relation between picture and frame is boldly exploited, the frame sometimes drawn as an actual window.

In an ebullient preface Dorat expresses the opinion that all fabulists are slaves, in mind if not in body. He eulogises La Fontaine none the less but criticises La Motte (see p. 16). He himself was not a particularly gifted writer, and this edition has been described by Bland as 'exquisite workmanship spent on worthless literature'. Dorat declared that his beasts had only been children of art whereas Marillier's were put back into nature (Portalis: *Les Dessinateurs d'illustrations au dix-huitième siècle* 1877).

22. THE TWO LAMPS

. . . 'Twas at a *Miser*'s cold Abode,
Two *chrystal Urns* survey'd the Road;
This shone (while That was void and damp)
Conscious of Oyl and Fire – a LAMP.
For Shew he plac'd them nothing loath,
But ah! th'Expence to light them both,
He saw by Calculation clear,
At This *per* Day was That *per* Year.
   The *beamless* Vase, when Night prevail'd,
Her Unimportance thus bewail'd:
Too partial Fate! why doom to me
This odious, dull Obscurity?
Here many a tedious Night I've hung,
Nor bless'd by old, nor prais'd by young,
To me scarce one kind Glance is given;
While like the Moon, that *Lamp of Heaven*,
My Sister of congenial Glass,
Wins all the Hearts of all that pass.
Suppose her Station they revere,
I boast the same exalted Sphere;
Do they with Awe her *Crown* behold,
Her Dress of blue, distinct with Gold?
These gave her not superior Fame,
Her Ornaments and mine the same.
'Tis not her easy Shape and Air,

Her swelling Bosom heavenly-clear,
Her smoother Polish, brighter Hue;
No; for in these we're hardly two.
   Yet while she sits triumphant by,
The *Cynosure** of every Eye,
I'm seen, if seen, with Scorn alone,
May fall unmiss'd, or stand unknown.
Speak, Dotards! speak, the Difference shew,
Or own Caprice rules all below.
   Sister, forbear, the other cry'd,
To tell the World you're mortify'd.
Envy no Votaries shall gain,
It scarce has Pity for its Pain.
   'Tis not indeed my fairer Frame, –
No native Excellence I clame;
'Tis not my Body's happier Mold,
More polish'd, pure, or rich with Gold:
In these one Character's our Due,
You fair as I, I frail as you.
And yet while you neglected sit,
Or but the Theme of taunting Wit,
I fix the Traveller's ardent Gaze,
Have all his Blessing, all his Praise.
   What can this different Treatment win?
Sure, Sister, 'tis THE LIGHT WITHIN.

**The Cynosure*: The North Star, by which Sailors steer
their Ships.

The Economy of Beauty; in a series of fables: addressed to the ladies. By Dr. Cosens. [Engraved by George Bickham, Isaac Taylor and others.] 4to. London, for J. Walter, 1777 [1776] 179–1889

The eighteenth century was the age of the literary fable, heralded by the original *Fables nouvelles* of Antoine Houdart de La Motte, whose *Discourse* established rules for the fable-writer and influenced among others 'Doddy', Johnson's friend Robert Dodsley (see also pp. 16–17). The immensely popular *Fables of Flowers for the Female Sex* by J.H. Wynne (1773) had been dedicated to the young Princess Charlotte, and Dr Cosens, on the evidence of an inserted manuscript letter, sent a pre-publication copy to this same royal child.

Nineteen of the twenty-two plates for Cosens' edifying fables – 'invented' or more precisely 'sketched' from Gillot – were copied from La Motte's handsome edition of 1719, an outstanding achievement of French Rococo book art. Three new illustrations were drawn and engraved by Isaac Taylor.

Taylor was at his best when working on a small scale, as in the title vignette to 'The Two Lamps', with its carefully delineated figures and exact rendering of the light and shade cast by the more effective lamp. From this period 'dates the gradual ascendancy of English engravers over their French masters' (Hammelmann 1952).

23. THE WOLF IN A SHEEPSKIN

A Wolf one day put on the skin of a sheep, and in this disguise for a long time kept devouring the lambs. But the Shepherd caught him and hung him from a high stake with the sheepskin still on him, to be a public spectacle and to serve as an example. The astonished neighbours asked him why he was hanging up his sheep in that way. You are wrong, he told them. It's the skin of a sheep, I can't deny, but it was hiding the body of a Wolf.

—— 🐑 ——

People should be judged neither by appearance nor by outward show, but by their behaviour and their deeds.

A. S. H.

Fables d'Ésope, representée en figures avec les explications et les principaux traits de sa vie. Gravée [after Barlow] par les meilleurs artistes. 8vo. A Paris, chez Henri Remoissenet [*c.* 1790?] 350-1889

Barlow's fable designs appear once again in a production of the Bewick era, intended for the education of children of both sexes and re-engraved with an accompanying French translation in the contemporary cursive script. Barlow's 1666 *Aesop* had texts in Latin, French and English (the first two by Robert Codrington, the last by Thomas Philipott), the edition of 1687 was 'newly translated' by the 'incomparable Astraea', Aphra Behn (and others), and in 1714 the pictures were finally united by Estienne Roger of Amsterdam with a French translation of L'Estrange's incomparable prose. Having attained the status of a classic throughout Europe, they are here combined with a less sophisticated text for the young reader.

Barlow's thirty-one plates to Aesop's *Life* were published for the first time in 1687 and for the last time in 1830. Designs for the *Life* have always descended separately from the various fable series (see pp. 13, 26); it was not illustrated by Gheeraerts and his successors. Barlow found models elsewhere: in Zainer, in Pieter van der Borcht (Antwerp, 1593) and possibly also in de Marnef (Paris, 1582). Though Aesop's clumsy figure strikes an incongruous note in the midst of the fantastic architecture and fashionably Baroque settings, Barlow's fabulist has become a personage, dignified rather than disadvantaged. His series was one of the most elaborate - and the grand finale: Aesop's *Life* was not illustrated again.

24. THE RAVENS, THE SEXTON, AND
THE EARTH-WORM

... Consider, man; weigh well thy frame;
The king, the beggar is the same.
Dust forms us all. Each breathes his day,
Then sinks into his native clay.

Beneath a venerable yew,
That in the lonely church-yard grew,
Two Ravens sat. In solemn croak
Thus one his hungry friend bespoke.

Methinks I scent some rich repast;
The savour strengthens with the blast;
Snuff then, the promis'd feast inhale;
I taste the carcase in the gale,
Near yonder trees, the farmer's steed,
From toil and daily drudg'ry freed,
Hath groan'd his last. A dainty treat!
To birds of taste delicious meat.

A Sexton, busy at his trade,
To hear their chat suspends his spade.
Death struck him with no farther thought,
Than merely as the fees he brought.
Was ever two such blund'ring fowls,
In brains and manners less than owls!
Blockheads, says he, learn more respect,
Know ye on whom you thus reflect?
In this same grave (who does me right,
Must own the work is strong and tight)
The 'Squire that yon fair hall possess'd,
To-night shall lay his bones at rest.
Whence could the gross mistake proceed?
The 'Squire was somewhat fat indeed.
What then? The meanest bird of prey
Such want of sense could ne'er betray;
For sure some diff'rence must be found
(Suppose the smelling organ sound)
In carcasses (say what we can)
Or where's the dignity of man?

With due respect to human race,
The Ravens undertook the case.
In such similitude of scent,
Man ne'er could think reflexions meant.
As epicures extol a treat,
And seem their sav'ry words to eat,
They prais'd dead horse, luxurious food,
The ven'son of the prescient brood.

The Sexton's indignation mov'd,

The mean comparison reprov'd;
The undiscerning palate blam'd,
Which two-legg'd carrion thus defam'd.

Reproachful speech from either side
The want of argument supply'd:
They rail, revile: as often ends
The contest of disputing friends.

Hold, says the Fowl; since human pride
With confutation ne'er comply'd,
Let's state the case, and then refer
The knotty point: for taste may err.

As thus he spoke, from out the mould
An Earth-worm, huge of size, unroll'd
His monstrous length. They strait agree
To choose him as their referee.
So to th'experience of his jaws,
Each states the merits of his cause.

He paus'd, and with a solemn tone,
Thus made his sage opinion known.

On carcases of ev'ry kind
This maw hath elegantly din'd;
Provok'd by luxury or need,
On beast, or fowl, or man, I feed;
Such small distinctions in the savour,
By turns I chuse the fancy'd flavour.
Yet I must own (that human beast)
A glutton is the rankest feast.
Man, cease this boast; for human pride
Hath various tracts to range beside.
The prince who kept the world in awe,
The judge whose dictate fix'd the law,
The rich, the poor, the great, the small,
Are levell'd. Death confounds 'em all.
Then think not that we reptiles share
Such cates, such elegance of fare:
The only true and real good
Of man was never vermin's food.
'Tis seated in th'immortal mind;
Virtue distinguishes mankind,
And that (as yet ne'er harbour'd here)
Mounts with his soul we know not where.
So, good-man Sexton, since the case
Appears with such a dubious face,
To neither I the cause determine.
For diff'rent tastes please diff'rent vermin.

FABLE XVI.

Fables by John Gay, with a Life of the Author. [After Stockdale's edition of the same year. Engraved by William Blake and others.] 8vo. London, by Darton & Harvey, for F. & C. Rivington [etc.], 1793.   Clements Bequest   L.1354-1948

Blake's twelve designs for Stockdale's prestigious 1793 edition of Gay's *Fables*, like his other early book illustrations, were taken from existing originals and done to earn a living. Instantly recognisable and hinting at the later visionary style, they are important among his minor works. Of the several artists who re-engraved the 1727 and 1738 plates (the latter reduced in size) after Kent, Wootton and Gravelot, Blake was the best-known, the most inventive and the most individual in expression, but even he resorted to the traditional composition and relationships of the figures. In this masterly re-creation of Gravelot the worm has been restored to more normal proportions.

25. THE CAMEL

At the Camel's first appearance in the world, most creatures were afraid to come near it, by reason of its unnatural bulk, and odd shape. But in process of time, they perceiving his gentleness, ventured to come near him. Soon after, finding that he was a harmless creature, they bridled him, and caused the very children to lead him up and down, and made him their game.

THE MORAL

Custom and use make things easy which at first view appeared hard, and that contemptible, which at first was dreadful.

THE REMARK

Use and custom are (I may say) a second nature. They make things easy and delightful, which at first view seemed strange, hard, and even frightful. Good nature is often abused: Men, as well as children, are apt to make their game, not only of inferiors, but also of superiors. Good-nature has made subjects turn too familiar even with their sovereigns.

Anon. (Glasgow, 1800)

Fables d'Ésope. Dédiées au Premier Consul Bonaparte. La traduction des fables est de J. B. Gail. Fol. A Paris, chez Basset, Beaublé (1801)   L.3415-1938

The grander fable editions were often dedicated to some member of the ruling class, young or old. In this large-format selection of nineteen fables, Napoleon Bonaparte is flattered by references to his Egyptian campaigns in a sprinkling of pyramids and camels, and in epigrammatic morals with an obvious political slant. After his defeats Napoleon was lampooned in caricatures depicting rattish opponents: a repetition of ancient themes from the *Cat-Mouse War*.

The engraved text, headed by Laurent Guyot's vignettes, is written out by Guillaume Montfort in copy-book 'lettres bâtardes' with elegant calligraphic flourishes.

La premiere fois qu'on vit un chameau,

les hommes surpris de sa grandeur

s'enfuirent effrayés. Peu de temps après,

ayant remarqué sa douceur, ils portèrent

la hardiesse jusqu'à lui donner un frein

et le faire conduire par des enfants.

—— Sens Moral. ——

L'habitude familiarise avec les objets terribles 9.

Guillaume - Montfort   Bariolle Sculpsit.

26. THE THUNNY AND THE DOLPHIN

A Thunny, closely pursued through the sea by a huge Dolphin, and within a moment of being swallowed by him, threw himself into the rift of a rock, where indeed his death was no less certain. The Dolphin, eager to secure his prey, flung himself impetuously after him, and shared the same fate. The Thunny looking round, and seeing the Dolphin at his last gasp, spent the last remains of his own breath in these words. Now my death gives me no uneasiness, since I see him, who was the cause of it, doom'd to die with me.

No torture we feel, by oppression brought low,
Like the triumph and joy of an insolent foe:
And no pleasure so sweet, when we cannot escape,
As to see our destroyer himself in the scrape.

APPLICATION

There is a kind of melancholy satisfaction in seeing the author of our miseries plunged into the same distressful circumstances with ourselves. It may be doubted indeed whether the giving way to the pleasure naturally arising in our breasts on such an occasion, is strictly justifiable: but surely they can with little justice reproach us, whose own guilt has in great measure been the cause of ours, and whose cruelty has urged us beyond human patience. However truly we may be censured, as yielding to the emotions of a revengeful temper, yet our crime has certainly this good effect, that it may be considered as a scourge in the hand of providence, to encrease the punishment of the haughty oppressor. Wherefore if nobler arguments should fail, an attention to their own peace of mind should persuade the great and powerful not to persecute their inferiors; for how can they endure their fall, if it should ever happen, when it is imbittered by the triumph of those very wretches, who were so lately the objects on which they exerted their cruelty and arrogance.

Charles Draper, 1774

Fables of Aesop, and Others: translated into English. With instructive applications: and a print before each fable. By Samuel Croxall, D.D. The twentieth edition. [First printed in 1722 by Tonson and Watts. Re-engraved after Elisha Kirkall.] London, for F.[,] C. & J. Rivington [etc.], 1818.   30.x.1877

Croxall meant his *Aesop* to supplant the 'pernicious principles' of L'Estrange's translation of thirty years before. Although the morals, indigestible and sometimes irrelevant, occupy half the book, it was published in up to two hundred editions and remained the most significant children's collection for the next century and a half – perhaps because for the first time in England every fable was illustrated, and because it was cheap.

Elisha Kirkall's 'adaptation' of traditional motifs in a series of one hundred and ninety-six oval metal cuts has been described as a landmark in the history of English book illustration (Hodnett 1976). Barlow, Chauveau and Le Clerc were the chief sources, but Kirkall developed the basic concepts in his own way, executing

FAB. LXIII. *The* THUNNY *and the* DOLPHIN.

both drawing and engraving himself. No English illustrator before Kirkall seems to have used the white-line method, but a forerunner, Pierre Eskrich, had engraved in relief on metal for his 1548 *Alciati*.

Improved printing techniques for relief engraving after 1800, together with John Lee's retouching of the plates, meant that later impressions were better than any since the mid-eighteenth century. Foreground contrast was now more strongly marked and there was an enhanced effect of depth, arising from Kirkall's habit of clearing white areas and working from black to white – which lent also a sculptural quality. Though they offered an economical alternative to expensive copper-plate books, the advantages of Kirkall's production methods were not fully appreciated in the nineteenth century. His example was followed not only by Bewick but by Blake and Calvert, and twentieth-century wood engravers adopted his techniques as a matter of course.

Charles Draper's rather more lively prose (published in 1774 with Kirkall's cuts) here replaces the loquacious Croxall, whose 'Hare and Tortoise' substitutes overleaf for Bewick.

27. THE HARE AND THE TORTOISE

A Hare insulted a Tortoise upon account of his slowness, and vainly boasted of her own great speed in running. Let us make a match, replied the Tortoise; I'll run with you five miles for five pounds, and the Fox yonder shall be the umpire of the race. The Hare agreed; and away they both started together. But the Hare, by reason of her exceeding swiftness, outran the Tortoise to such a degree, that she made a jest of the matter; and finding herself a little tired, squatted in a tuft of fern that grew by the way, and took a nap; thinking, that if the Tortoise went by, she could at any time fetch him up, with all the ease imaginable. In the mean while the Tortoise came jogging on, with a slow but continued motion; and the Hare, out of a too great security and confidence of victory, oversleeping herself, the Tortoise arrived at the end of the race first.

THE APPLICATION

Industry and application to business make amends for the want of a quick and ready wit. Hence it is, that the victory is not always to the strong, nor the race to the swift. Men of fine parts are apt to despise the drudgery of business; but, by affecting to show the superiority of their genius, upon many occasions, they run into too great an extreme the other way; and the administration of their affairs is ruined through idleness and neglect. What advantage has a man from the fertility of his invention, and the vivacity of his imagination, unless his resolutions are executed with a suitable and uninterrupted rapidity? In short, your men of wit and fire, as they are called, are oftentimes sots, slovens, and lazy fellows: they are generally proud and conceited to the last degree; and in the main, not the fittest persons for either conversation or business. Such is their vanity, they think the sprightliness of their humour inconsistent with a plain, sober way of thinking and speaking, and able to atone for all the little neglects of their business and persons. But the world will not be thus imposed upon; the man who would gain the esteem of others, and make his own fortune, must be one that carries his point effectually, and finishes his course without swerving or loitering. Men of dull parts and a slow apprehension, assisted by a continued diligence, are more likely to attain this, than your brisk retailers of wit, with their affected spleen and indolence. And if business be but well done, no matter whether it be done by the sallies of a refined wit, or the considering head of a plain, plodding man.

Samuel Croxall, 20 edn, 1818

The Fables of Aesop, and Others, with designs on wood, by Thomas Bewick. [Imperial edition.] Newcastle, by E. Walker, for T. Bewick & Son, 1818. L. 1061-1969

The last traces of Gheeraerts' influence are seen in Bewick's fable-books, in which many of the designs derive from Kirkall's cuts to Croxall's *Aesop* (p. 85), themselves based on Barlow (p. 63) and on Chauveau's illustrations to the first *La Fontaine* (1668). Bewick admired, revived and perfected Kirkall's technique of white-line engraving, executing his designs on more durable endgrain boxwood blocks.

According to the practice of Le Clerc and Kirkall in their Aesop illustrations, he chose a format suited to the headpiece – horizontal ovals disciplined within strict rectangular frames.

Bewick's first fable series (to John Gay) appeared in 1779. Next came the 1784 and 1814 collections and finally his own version of 1818, the illustrations for which he drew during a long convalescence in 1812. Several tailpieces represent the headstones of fabulists' graves and the last his brother's funeral. Bewick himself compiled and edited one hundred and eighty-eight prose fables from English authors of the seventeenth and eighteenth centuries, but did *not* include Croxall – although he considered that Croxall's *Aesop* had 'led hundreds of young men into the paths of wisdom and rectitude'. Addressing the 'Youth of the British Isles', he seems conscious of a new responsibility on the part of author and illustrator. His exhaustive and exhausting moral applications stress the virtues of patriotism, modesty, industry, integrity and so forth. Here a Croxall text has been chosen for 'The Hare and the Tortoise' in preference to Bewick's more pedestrian version.

The 1784 *Select Fables* had helped to establish Bewick's reputation, but his work for this edition was apparently a disappointment to him since many of the subjects could not be studied at first hand. The animals, even if often derivative, are no less minutely and intensely observed than in the zoological drawings for his *History of British Birds* (1797), and again we are made aware of the primacy of the animal specialist in fable illustration.

28. THE EARTHEN POT AND THE IRON POT

An iron pot proposed
  To an earthen pot a journey.
The latter was opposed,
  Expressing the concern he
Had felt about the danger
Of going out a ranger.
He thought the kitchen hearth
The safest place on earth
For one so very brittle.
For thee, who art a kettle,
And hast a tougher skin,
There's nought to keep thee in.
I'll be thy body-guard,
  Replied the iron pot;
If any thing that's hard
  Should threaten thee a jot,
Between you I will go,
And save thee from the blow.

This offer him persuaded.
The iron pot paraded
Himself as guard and guide
Close at his cousin's side.
Now, in their tripod way,
They hobble as they may;
And eke together bolt
At every little jolt, —
Which gives the crockery pain;
  But presently his comrade hits
  So hard, he dashes him to bits,
Before he can complain.

Take care that you associate
With equals only, lest your fate
Between these pots should find its mate.

Elizur Wright, junior, 1841

Fables de La Fontaine. Édition illustrée par J. J. Grandville. Paris, H. Fournier aîné, 1838. Townshend Bequest 9.x.1868

One of the great French caricaturists in the shadow of Daumier (Doderer 1971), Grandville provoked sharp protests from leading critics of the day by his bold approach to this best-selling classic, condemned by Taine (1853) as a 'vulgar carnival'. The one hundred and twenty woodcuts, published in 1838 and much reprinted, became the first outstanding *La Fontaine* series of this century – though they were less popular in England than in France, where the September laws of 1835 had forbidden political satire.

The usual fable pattern is reversed, in that Grandville's animals turn into human beings. Their clothing and conduct betray their social standing (as with Bennett, p. 99); in this he faithfully records La Fontaine's intentions, rarely departing from the text. Only by their heads are they linked with the fable motifs – but then he transforms them into animals again by restoring their own characteristics. Sometimes his fantasy borders on the surreal, as in the case of these humanised pots.

To Grandville, action and decor are less important than disguise and gesture. The rôle of nature is a subordinate one, and many of his fables are set in the city. Grandville was the first to tell the whole story, and like Doré (see p. 29) often heightened the dramatic effect by telling it in two ways at once. The principal action is mirrored in an allegorical, almost emblematic interpretation, or in a secondary scene from the human comedy played out in the background.

LE POT DE TERRE ET LE POT DE FER

29. GOOSE

'Goose, what a poor little creature are you,
To have no stockings and never a shoe.'
Goose
'You might certainly give me a pair;
But would they be proper for me to wear?
Would not the beautiful things be soiled,
If I went in water, and wetted, and spoil'd?'

The nearest brook was his favourite place;
He went splashing through it with thoughtful pace,
Walking or swimming its surface o'er,
And little caring for anything more.
He stay'd in the water the whole day through,
And never thought once of stocking or shoe.

Translated by H. W. Dulcken, 1858

Noch f[ü]nfzig Fabeln für Kinder [by Wilhelm Hey]. In Bildern, gezeichnet von Otto Speckter.
[New edition.] Hamburg, bei Friedrich Perthes [*c.*1840]   Guy Little Bequest   L.5190-1961

The animal verses by the Thuringian pastor and teacher Wilhelm Hey, embodiments of the sentimental 'fables' in vogue at the time, were originally devised not for publication but to cheer up his children, sick with measles. Hey's friend Perthes commissioned Otto Speckter to illustrate with lithographs the anonymous book edition of 1833 (for publication Hey added a second verse to each fable) and also its 1837 sequel, in which the moralising side was made more obvious. An English woodcut edition came out in 1858.

Speckter had a singular gift for drawing animals, and this was one of his earliest and finest achievements - followed later by illustrations to Andersen and other fairy tales. Both text and illustrations had an international appeal, eventually becoming known as the 'Hey-Specktersche Fabeln' since the two colleagues worked together in such close association. Edition followed edition, and Speckter's pictures were soon coarsened by the intervention of mediocre draughtsmen. He was so incensed by their poor execution that he consigned all copies sent him to the stove.

Hey's fables were much esteemed as a literary and aesthetic model in elementary-school teaching and gave rise to an educational treatise edited by Karl Kehr, entitled *Der Anschauungs-Unterricht für Haus und Schule auf Grundlage der Hey-Speckterschen Fabeln* (1883). Hey's situations are taken from the real world, seen through rose-coloured spectacles. The innate quality of each creature is clearly brought out so as to foster a love of animals; this trusting relationship between beast and man is meant to reflect that between man and God. The fables however speak not to reason but to the emotions - depicting accurately drawn but merely fetching animals, simplifying both action and language, and sweetening the pill to such an extent that the old fable types have disappeared. All that is left is a touching moral tale.

30. THE GRASSHOPPER AND THE ANT

The gay grasshopper having sung
All the sunny season long,
Was unprovided and brought low,
When the north wind began to blow;
Had not a scrap of worm or fly,
Hunger and want began to cry;
Never was creature more perplex'd,
She call'd upon her neighbour ant,
And humbly pray'd her just to grant
Some grain till August next;
I'll pay, she said, if I exist,
Both principal and interest,
Honor of insects – and that's tender.
The ant, however, is no lender;
That is her least defective side:
But hark ye pray Miss borrower, she cried,
What were ye doing in fine weather?
Singing . . . I hope there's no offence,
To every comer day and night together:
Singing! I'm glad of that, why now then dance.

Robert Thomson, 1806

The Child[']s Illuminated Fable-Book. [Fables taken from La Fontaine. Twelve colour plates lithographed by Woods & Co.] London, William Smith [1847]   17.iv.1874

In a fashionable imitation of mediaeval manuscript illumination, the fable-characters are contained within small compartments, escaping with the fruits and flowers of their environment into borders entwined with foliage.

'The Ant and the Grasshopper' is the first in La Fontaine's twelve books of fables: Sébastien Chamfort, author of the *Éloge de La Fontaine* (1774), calls it the weakest! This cautionary tale of improvidence demands special treatment on account of the small size and relative unfamiliarity of the dramatis personae. From 1542 to 1811 the basic design remains the same, with the insects in the foreground – the ant emerging from its refuge in the stump of a tree – and beyond it, a landscape with figures. A few years later, Grandville's ant is dressed as a petit-bourgeois housewife and his grasshopper as a bedraggled travelling musician, while Doré completely metamorphoses Grandville's insects into their human counterparts.

(See colour illustration p. 17)

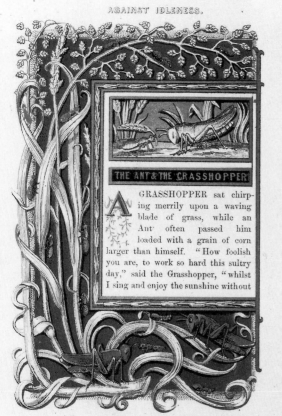

THE ANT & THE GRASSHOPPER

A GRASSHOPPER sat chirping merrily upon a waving blade of grass, while an Ant often passed him loaded with a grain of corn larger than himself. "How foolish you are, to work so hard this sultry day," said the Grasshopper, "whilst I sing and enjoy the sunshine without

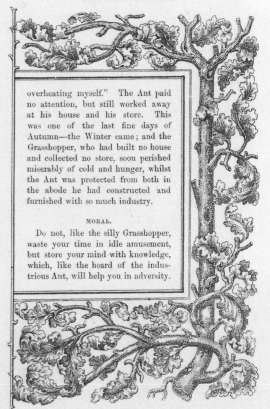

overheating myself." The Ant paid no attention, but still worked away at his house and his store. This was one of the last fine days of Autumn—the Winter came; and the Grasshopper, who had built no house and collected no store, soon perished miserably of cold and hunger, whilst the Ant was protected from both in the abode he had constructed and furnished with so much industry.

MORAL.

Do not, like the silly Grasshopper, waste your time in idle amusement, but store your mind with knowledge, which, like the hoard of the industrious Ant, will help you in adversity.

31. THE THREE HERONS

Feeling hungry towards evening, three Herons were watching for their prey in a pond. They demanded little enough; just three fish – to each according to his taste. Heaven sent them the fish. The first Heron seized a roach: happy bird! Happy? far from it – he wanted the bream which the second Heron had just snapped up, and the latter was lamenting a pickerel which the third was holding in his beak. As for the third Heron, he said to himself: 'A carp would have been more to my taste'. We see here our jealous desires revealed indeed: no one is content with the share allotted him by fate.

A.S.H.

Fables de S. Lavalette. Illustrées de nouvelles eaux-fortes par Grandville. Troisième édition, revue et augmentée. Paris, J. Hetzel, 1847.   L. 5610-1970

Both in his *La Fontaine* (pp. 88-9) and in his illustrations for Sourdille de Lavalette, Grandville makes a complete break with the early Aesop cycles. Lavalette's fables (some familiar and borrowed) appeared in 1828 and again in 1841 with twenty-four plates by Grandville, augmented by eight more for the edition of 1847, the year of Grandville's death. A line or two of text was engraved beneath each picture.

Grandville shares with Gheeraerts and Bewick their mastery of animal drawing and their exact and painstaking detail, but he is rather more fascinated than his predecessors by the similarities of animals to humans. Much of his other work (for instance the *Métamorphoses du jour; ou, les hommes à têtes de bêtes* of 1829) shows humans in the guise of animals, so it seems quite natural for him to portray animals in human attitudes.

Il est souvent de sa mort que le pecheur lui donne

32. THE STAG AT THE POOL

A Stag one summer's day came to a pool to quench his thirst, and as he stood drinking he saw his form reflected in the water. 'What beauty and strength,' said he, 'are in these horns of mine; but how unseemly are these weak and slender feet!' While he was thus criticising, after his own fancies, the form which Nature had given him, the huntsmen and hounds drew that way. The feet, with which he had found so much fault, soon carried him out of the reach of his pursuers; but the horns, of which he was so vain, becoming entangled in a thicket, held him till the hunters again came up to him, and proved the cause of his death.

Look to use before ornament.

Aesop's Fables: a new version, chiefly from original sources, by the Rev. Thomas James, M.A. With more than one hundred illustrations designed by John Tenniel. [Engraved on wood by Leopold Martin.] London, John Murray, 1848.   2. v. 1854

The young Tenniel's flair for animal drawing is evident in the exquisite but mannered accuracy of his *Aesop's Fables* (in 'Murray's Reading for the Rail Series') which furthered his career and his fortune. On the strength of this book he was employed by Doyle, and then by *Punch* – where his animals become human caricatures.

In making his paraphrase of old and new English sources James grafted in conventional English sayings, removing contemporary traits from the morals and leaving only their universal wisdom. Tenniel collaborated closely with the compiler as later with Lewis Carroll, but his pictures add little to the story. Most noticeable is their decorative function, especially where the page incorporates the text (see also *The Child's Illuminated Fable-Book*, pp. 17, 93).

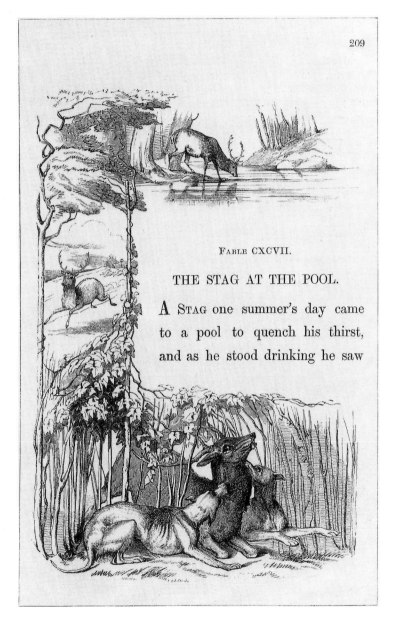

FABLE CXCVII.

THE STAG AT THE POOL.

A STAG one summer's day came to a pool to quench his thirst, and as he stood drinking he saw

33. THE DOG IN THE MANGER

A churlish, pampered Cur, who had a comfortable place in a gentleman's well-filled Manger, would from thence snap and snarl to frighten off all poor beasts of draught and burden who passed that way – driven by the hardness of the time of year to beg for provender they could not earn by labour in the fields. This Dog wanted for nothing himself, and yet took an ill-natured pleasure in keeping poor famishing creatures from many a meal, which, but for his officious yelping, they might have enjoyed from his Master's bounty.

MORAL

There would be sunshine in many a poor man's house, but for officious, go-between window-shutters.

The Fables of Aesop and Others Translated into Human Nature. [By Charles H. Bennett.] Designed and drawn on the wood by Charles H. Bennett. Engraved by Swain. London, W. Kent & Co, 1857. L. 5632-1961 (Guy Little Bequest), 585-1887

Some of Bennett's best work was done for his once popular and now rare fable-book, aimed at older children, from which he eradicated traditional animal stereo-types. As with Grandville the animals have human bodies, behave like humans and are fully clothed. In these elegant drawing-room settings, dress indicates position in society. Only the heads remain beast-like. A certain sophistication is demanded of the reader, who needs to be familiar not only with Aesop and with animal nature but also with human nature and fashionable London life.

The twenty-two fables were furnished with woodcuts engraved by Swain, like Bennett a *Punch* artist and much involved with children's books. In the hand-tinted edition Bennett anticipates with his use of colour the great illustrators of the next generation – Caldecott, Crane and Greenaway – but these three have none of his sinister undertones.

(See colour illustration p. 20)

THE DOG IN THE MANGER.

34. THE TOWN RAT
AND THE COUNTRY RAT

A Rat from town, a country Rat
    Invited in the civilest way;
For dinner there was just to be
    Ortolans and an entremet.

Upon a Turkey carpet soft
    The noble feast at last was spread;
I leave you pretty well to guess
    The merry, pleasant life they led.

Gay the repast, for plenty reigned,
    Nothing was wanting to the fare;
But hardly had it well begun
    Ere chance disturbed the friendly pair.

A sudden racket at the door
    Alarmed them, and they made retreat;

The City Rat was not the last,
    His comrade followed fast and fleet.

The noise soon over, they returned,
    As rats on such occasions do;
'Come,' said the liberal citizen,
    'And let us finish our ragout.'

'Not a crumb more,' the rustic said;
    'To-morrow you shall dine with me;
Don't think me jealous of your state,
    Or all your royal luxury;

'But then I eat so quiet at home,
    And nothing dangerous is near;
Good-bye, my friend, I have no love
    For pleasure when it's mixed with fear.'

The Fables of La Fontaine. Translated into English verse by Walter Thornbury. With [wood-engraved] illustrations by Gustave Doré. London & New York, Cassell, Petter & Galpin [1868]   30. ix. 1871

Inspired by Grandville and his satirical vein, though less adept as an animal artist, Doré more daringly than perhaps any other illustrator before Chagall blends diverse facets of La Fontaine's art, from the epic to the burlesque. The large print and generous format, especially of the English edition, are evidence that he intended these fables for the juvenile market – an impression belied by stark scenes and lowering landscapes in the dark mood of his *Inferno* designs.

Rich but sombre interiors reveal an Oudryesque taste for luxury against which the often tragic dénouement is played out. For Doré and La Fontaine, men and animals alike are doomed to suffer, at the mercy of an indifferent and menacing nature. But Doré betrays a Romantic empathy with the smaller animals and so with man, equally helpless. Even the field of view is that of a small animal – a frog's perspective. The plates and knives seem huge and dangerous, and the rats are about to spring out at us from the table.

The fable of the Town Rat (or Mouse) and the Country Rat has been a favourite from early times, sometimes interpreted – by James I and L'Estrange amongst others – as demonstrating the advantages of a quiet country life. To Pope it was a celebration of liberty, that compensation for minor misfortunes:

Give me again my holly tree,
A crust of bread and liberty!

(*Imitations of Horace*, Book II, Satire VI)

35. THE EAGLE AND THE CROW

A Crow watched an Eagle swoop with a majestic air from a neighbouring cliff upon a flock of Sheep, and carry away a Lamb in his talons. The whole thing looked so graceful and so easy withal, that the Crow at once proceeded to imitate it, and pouncing upon the back of the largest and fattest Ram he could see, he tried to make off with it. He found not only that he could not move the Ram, but that his claws got so entangled in the animal's fleece, that he could not get away himself. He therefore became an easy prey to the Shepherd, who, coming up at the time, caught him, cut his wings, and gave him to his children for a plaything.

Aesop's Fables. Illustrated by Ernest Griset. With text based chiefly upon Croxall, La Fontaine, and L'Estrange. Revised and re-written by J. B. Rundell. London, Cassell, Petter & Galpin [1869]   Guy Little Bequest   L. 5006-1961

Griset's highly-regarded Aesop designs were his first major work; for the 1893 edition extra drawings accompanied the additional one hundred and thirty fables in prose and verse. This French-born artist, best-known for his natural history illustration and caricatures of Darwin, made a name for himself as well with his contributions to *Punch*. Griset followed Doré, choosing the same fables and combining full-page 'painterly' plates with small headpiece vignettes – again often freer in style than the plates – in the text. Some of the wood engravings have his customary light and whimsical touch; others are powerful and macabre in Doré's manner, with similar chiaroscuro contrasts.

Nearly all Griset's drawings represent animals in a state of nature: usually only the evil beasts are clothed, and never the birds. Slaughter and death continually recur, and guilt is visited upon the principals.

36. THE TRAVELLERS AND THE BEAR

Two men were travelling together through a wood, which was much infested with wild beasts; so they agreed to stand by each other in case of any sudden danger. They had not proceeded far before a savage Bear rushed out upon them. One of them, forgetting his companion and his promises, immediately ran to a tree and climbed up into its branches; the other, thus left to himself, felt that he had no chance against the Bear, and remembering that he had heard that that animal will not touch a dead body, he threw himself flat on his face, and pretended to be dead. The Bear came up to him as he thus lay, smelt and sniffed at him all over, and at length, feeling satisfied that there was no life in the body before him, walked back again into the wood. Upon this the coward descended from his hiding-place, and with a smile asked his companion what it was that the Bear had whispered to him; 'for I noticed,' said he, 'that he put his mouth very close to your ear.' 'Why,' replied the other, 'he gave me this very sensible piece of advice, – never to trust those who in the hour of trial refuse to stand by their friends.'

A false friend is worse than an open foe.

The Children's Picture Fable-Book. Containing one hundred and sixty fables. With sixty illustrations by Harrison Weir. [New edition. Engraved on wood by John Greenaway.] London, George Routledge & Sons [1872] 6.i.1873

Fables were always included in reading books as a matter of course, and animal moral tales refurbished or copied *ad nauseam* throughout the nineteenth century. Aesop, over-used, had lost his spontaneity but came back to life with the inventiveness of interpreters such as Bennett and Crane (see pp. 20, 21, 99, 109).

Several children's editions of Aesop such as this large-print volume in 'Routledge's Album Series' were given new energy by Harrison Weir's sensitive wood engravings, first printed in 1860. Weir's animals, completely natural, do not pretend to be human but their faces and attitudes on the whole express admirably the emotions of each incident.

THE TRAVELLERS AND THE BEAR.

37. THE COCK AND THE JEWEL

A Barn-door Cock while scratching up his dunghill came upon a Jewel. 'Oh, why,' said he, 'should I find this glistening thing? If some jeweller had found it he would have been beside himself with joy at the thought of its value: but to me it is of no manner of use, nor do I care one jot about it; why, I would rather have one grain of barley than all the jewels in the world.'

Some of Aesop's Fables with Modern Instances, shewn in designs by Randolph Caldecott, from new translations by Alfred Caldecott, M.A. London, Macmillan & Co, 1883. Guy Little Bequest L. 5614-1961

Caldecott, another *Punch* illustrator, started work on his twofold Aesop designs in 1878; the texts were translated mainly from Greek collections by his younger brother, a Cambridge philologist and later Dean of King's College, London. 'The Translations aim at replacing the florid style of our older English versions, and the stilted harshness of more modern ones, by a plainness and terseness more nearly like the character of the originals' (A.C.). Alfred had hoped to make an authentic translation but Randolph intervened, modifying his version with traditional English retellings – the drawings had after all preceded the text. The word 'Some' implied that other collections were planned, but this first one did not sell as well as anticipated. A few fables were printed in the *English Illustrated Magazine*; others were never published. Many of the preliminary sketches and abandoned drawings are in the Victoria and Albert Museum.

We see here Caldecott's 'marvellous power in expressing a story in a few lines' (Pennell: *Pen Drawing and Pen Draughtsmen* 1889). At the suggestion of his engraver, J. D. Cooper, and with Bennett's example before him, Caldecott added to each straightforward fable picture in place of the time-honoured moral ending a humorous contemporary scene with witty social or political allusions to middle-class life. It is often debatable whether the 'modern instance' does not in fact leave the more lasting impression.

After Bewick's time a growing artistic self-consciousness caused fable-books to be known not by the author's or editor's name (as with Ogilby or Croxall) but by the name of the illustrator: Bennett's or Caldecott's *Aesop*, Grandville's or Doré's *La Fontaine*. In the case of Caldecott – and later, of Rackham – this newfound confidence occasionally extended to self-caricature.

The sign reads:
TRAVELLER'S
REST
J. JONES
BEERSELLER
BOOK

38. THE TREES AND THE AXE

A Woodman went into the forest and begged of the Trees the favour of a handle for his Axe. The principal Trees at once agreed to so modest a request, and unhesitatingly gave him a young ash sapling, out of which he fashioned the handle he desired. No sooner had he done so than he set to work to fell the noblest Trees in the wood. When they saw the use to which he was putting their gift, they cried, 'Alas! alas! We are undone, but we are ourselves to blame. The little we gave has cost us all: had we not sacrificed the rights of the ash, we might ourselves have stood for ages.'

V. S. Vernon Jones, 1912

The Baby's Own Aesop, being the fables condensed in rhyme with portable morals pictorially pointed by Walter Crane. Engraved & printed in colours by Edmund Evans. London & New York, George Routledge & Sons, 1887. L.2621-1980

Walter Crane in a letter to Caldecott (1882) confesses to being 'sad about a lost baby at present': the Society for Promoting Christian Knowledge had just returned his proposal for a fable-book. Caldecott hesitated to exploit the S.P.C.K.'s interest in his own fables and so delayed their publication (see pp. 106-7). The Society eventually imported a La Fontaine translation illustrated by Boutet de Monvel; Crane's fables were printed by Routledge.

These compact verse fables in limerick form were based on the manuscript of *The Wisdom of Aesop*, lent to Crane by his master, the engraver and radical journalist W. J. Linton. Crane's are among the earliest Aesop illustrations to use photoetching, a technique which simplified the reproduction of drawings. The strong outline and flat tints could easily be adapted to ceramic tiles; the designs were indeed used both for tiles and for a household frieze.

Crane was a driving force behind the Arts and Crafts Exhibition Society. Influenced by Japanese art and revolting against crude Victorian 'toy books', he pioneered the new picture book. Like Caldecott he demanded high standards and was similarly upheld in his ideals by the excellent colour work of Edmund Evans. The decoration as opposed to the illustration of books absorbed Crane more and more; he came to 'subordinate everything to the design of the printed page' (Lewis: *The Twentieth Century Book* 1967).

The Baby's Own Aesop was the least successful of Crane's 'Triplets': the name given when it was published together with two earlier quartos, *The Baby's Opera* and *The Baby's Bouquet*, in 1899. Adopting the square format of these nursery song anthologies – perhaps with tiles in mind – Crane fills each page with intricate subsidiary ornament, making no concessions to the unsophisticated eye of a child. Revolting against 'the despotism of the facts' (Darton 1982), he did not allow himself to be fettered by the text, which is not particularly suitable for children. Some fables exhibit a savage streak and the moral is not always apparent.

(See colour illustration p. 21)

THE TREES & THE WOODMAN

THE TREES ask of Man
what he lacks;
"One bit, just to handle my axe?"
All he asks — well and good;
But he cuts down the wood
So well does he handle his axe!

" GIVE ME AN INCH & I'LL TAKE AN
ELL "

39. THE OAK AND THE REED

The oak said one day to the reed: 'You certainly have cause for complaint against Nature. Even a wren is a heavy burden to you, and the slightest breeze which chances to ripple the surface of the water makes you hang down your head – while my forehead, like some proud mountain, is not content just to counter the sun's blazing rays but defies the fury of the tempest. To you all winds are like the North Wind; to me they are merely gentle Zephyrs. If you had only grown in the shelter of the foliage with which I cover this neighbourhood, you would suffer less – I should defend you from the storm. But usually you grow on the marshes which fringe the realms of the wind. It seems to me that Nature treats you quite unjustly.' 'Your compassion', the bush answered him, 'arises from a natural benevolence – but do not be anxious on my behalf. The winds are less dreadful to me than to you. I bend and do not break. Till now you have resisted their fearful buffetings without giving way. But let us wait for the final outcome.' As he speaks these words, there erupts in fury from the uttermost horizon the fiercest child that the North has yet brought forth. The tree stands firm, the reed bends. The wind redoubles its efforts, and with such success that it uproots the one whose head had soared to the Heavens and whose feet had reached to the Kingdom of the Dead.

A.S.H.

Choix de fables de La Fontaine. Illustrées par un groupe des meilleurs artistes de Tokio, sous la direction de P. Barboutau. [Large paper edition.] Tokyo, Tsoukidji [Tsukiji Printing Workshop]; Paris, Flammarion, 1894. 278-9-1895

This Oriental interpretation of Western fables was carried out by celebrated Tokyo artists of the day, including Kajita Hanko (opposite) and Kanō Tomonobu (p. 25), in the style of seventeenth-century Japanese wood engravings and in a spirit of deliberate archaism (see also Gooden, pp. 122–3). Claris de Florian's fables received the same treatment a year later. The twenty-eight fables selected nearly all have animal subjects – whose symbolic significance is surely often very different to Eastern eyes. They inspired illustrations serene in colour and harmonious in contour which echo La Fontaine's sensitivity to the natural world. Animals and birds are depicted as part of their surroundings, but rarely are we made aware of the desperate struggle for existence.

(See colour illustration p. 25)

40. THE KID AND THE WOLF

A Kid strayed from the flock and was chased by a Wolf. When he saw he must be caught he turned round and said to the Wolf, 'I know, sir, that I can't escape being eaten by you: and so, as my life is bound to be short, I pray you let it be as merry as may be. Will you not play me a tune to dance to before I die?' The Wolf saw no objection to having some music before his dinner: so he took out his pipe and began to play, while the Kid danced before him. Before many minutes were passed the dogs who guarded the flock heard the sound and came up to see what was going on. They no sooner clapped eyes on the Wolf than they gave chase and drove him away. As he ran off, he turned and said to the Kid, 'It's what I thoroughly deserve: my trade is the butcher's, and I had no business to turn piper to please you.'

Aesop's Fables. A new translation by V.S. Vernon Jones, with an introduction by G.K. Chesterton and illustrations by Arthur Rackham. London, Heinemann (printed by Ballantyne Press); New York, Doubleday, Page & Co, 1912. L. 2589-1972

Rackham's *Aesop* - a small book with a large sale - was a recreation for him from the more solemn art of his designs for Wagner's *Ring*, and intended to amuse. It was much liked by children and adults.

Watercolour plates alternate with black-and-white text illustrations, some full-page. The latter in particular reveal a feeling for abstract pattern and a talent for individualising animals through their faces and 'hands' (Gettings). The theory that creatures have human traits is further developed in Rackham's benign satire, which unmasks animal qualities dormant - or sometimes all too obvious - in human beings. In this world where men, beasts and inanimate objects seem to coexist and converse quite spontaneously, Rackham's behatted floating pots are far less startling and fantastic than Grandville's 'pot de terre' and 'pot de fer' lurching along to their ruin.

(See colour illustration p. 28)

41. THE CROW AND THE FOX

Master Crow, perched in a tree, was holding a cheese in his beak. Master Fox, attracted by the scent, addressed him something like this: 'Good-day to you, Lord Crow, how handsome you are and what an excellent bird to be sure! In truth, if your singing is as fine as your feathers, you must be a very Phoenix among the birds of these woods'. The Crow, beside himself with delight at the Fox's words and eager to show off his voice, opened wide his beak and dropped his prize. The Fox snapped it up and said: 'My dear Sir, you must learn that all flatterers live at the expense of those who swallow their words. I've no doubt this lesson's worth a cheese to you'. The Crow, crestfallen and ashamed, swore – too late – that he wouldn't be taken in like that again.

A.S.H.

Fables de La Fontaine. (Avec images de André Hellé. Nancy, Berger-Levrault) 1922.   Presented by J. Gamber   L. 1132–1930

At the other end of the spectrum from nineteenth-century profusion is Hellé's pared-down unsentimentality, somewhat reminiscent of Lovat Fraser's manner. André Hellé painted views of Paris and its people, and decors for the Théâtre des Arts before specialising in book and magazine illustration, mainly humorous and for the young – and attempting, unusually for his time, to realise a milieu for the child. Children's rooms with names like 'Chambre de Cendrillon' and 'L'Arche de Noé' were exhibited at the Salon d'Automne, each with its frieze opening a window on the life of the imagination. Creating with C.-E. Carlègle a new aesthetic of the toy, Hellé used vivid tints, concentrating on suggestion and silhouette at the expense of detail. In the First World War he devised new methods of camouflage.

Hellé attracted public attention above all with his theatre decors, designing costumes and scenery for Debussy's ballet 'La Boîte à Joujoux'; a book edition came out in 1913. He supervised the overall design of his children's albums and for some, such as Grosses bêtes et petites bêtes (1911) with its imaginary animals, he composed both story and picture. By order of the Ministry of Public Instruction he produced the 'Imagerie scolaire', a series of genre pictures to be distributed in schools – moral advice given with tongue in cheek.

In the pochoirs for Fables de La Fontaine (later reprinted in the U.S.A.), the panache of Hellé's line with its characteristic reduction to essentials is enlivened by splashes of clear, strong colour. So plainly does he communicate the eager angle of the fox's head in a few spare and dashing strokes that the picture alone almost tells the story.

(See colour illustration p. 24)

LE CORBEAU
ET LE RENARD

Maître Corbeau, sur un arbre perché,
tenait en son bec un fromage.
Maître Renard, par l'odeur alléché,
lui tint à peu près ce langage :
— Hé! bonjour, Monsieur du Corbeau!
Que vous êtes joli! que vous me semblez beau!

42. THE PIPING FISHERMAN

A fisherman who could play very well on the pipes took his pipes and nets and went down to the sea, where he stood upon an outstanding rock and began to play; for he thought that the fish would come readily out to hear his sweet music. But finding himself after much labour none the better off, he laid aside the pipes, reached for his casting-net, threw it into the water and got a fine catch of fishes. Then throwing them out from the net upon the shore, and watching them twist and turn about, 'You perverse creatures,' said he, 'when I piped to you, you would not dance; but as soon as my playing is over, 'tis that and nothing else with you.'

[Seven Fables of Aesop.] (The engravings by David Jones. The translations by W. H. Shewring. London, Lanston Monotype Corporation, 1928.) L. 4635-1934

Stanley Morison commissioned from David Jones seven small plates for *Seven Fables of Aesop*, a type-specimen of Victor Scholderer's New Hellenic type, a 'singularly handsome fount of great legibility and distinction' (*Fleuron* VI, 1928). It was cut by the Lanston Monotype Corporation, a commercial printing firm which occasionally published under its own imprint. This rare edition was limited ostensibly to one hundred and fifty copies; only thirty-five or possibly fifty seem to have been printed. Another edition was planned by Douglas Cleverdon but had to be abandoned. The illustration shown appeared as a specimen plate in the 'édition de luxe' of *Fleuron* VI. All the plates were presumed lost in the Blitz on Fetter Lane in May 1941, which destroyed the premises of the Monotype Corporation.

Jones worked mainly in watercolour with much use of drawn outline. Before 1927, when Cleverdon invited him to engrave on copper a series of illustrations to *The Rime of the Ancient Mariner* (published in 1929), he had engraved fewer than a dozen copper plates. They included bookplates, one of St Francis and the Wolf for W. H. Shewring, who translated these fables as well as Eric Gill's explicit introduction to his book of engravings – into Latin prose, 'thus circumventing sniggering illiterates' (Cleverdon 1983). Jones had done the title page to Shewring's 1930 book of poems. Copper engravings were considered too for the *Morte D'Arthur* of Malory and for his own *In Parenthesis*, but illness put an end to both projects. From 1926 Jones embarked on a number of animal pictures, a line of development which can be traced from *Aesop* and the *Ancient Mariner* to the *Guenever* of 1940 and beyond. His fable-book was dedicated to Desmond Chute, who had taught him the art of engraving on wood and copper.

David Jones, a versatile artist and writer, was an associate of Eric Gill and a mystic in the tradition of Blake. As one himself absorbed by myth, Jones inscribed his fables to 'Aesop the myth-maker'.

3. Ἁλιεὺς αὐλητής.

Ἁλιεὺς αὐλητικῆς ἔμπειρος, ἀναλαβὼν τοὺς αὐλοὺς καὶ τὰ δίκτυα παρεγένετο εἰς τὴν θάλασσαν, καὶ στὰς ἐπί τινος προβλήματος πέτρας τὸ μὲν πρῶτον ᾖδε, νομίζων αὐτομάτους πρὸς τὴν ἡδυφωνίαν τοὺς ἰχθύας ἐξελεύσεσθαι. ὡς δ’ αὐτοῦ ἐπὶ πολὺ διατεινομένου οὐδὲν πέρας ἠνύετο, ἀποθέμενος τοὺς αὐλοὺς ἀνείλετο τὸ ἀμφίβληστρον, καὶ βαλὼν κατὰ τοῦ ὕδατος πολλοὺς ἰχθύας ἤγρευσεν. ἐκβαλὼν δ’ αὐτοὺς ἀπὸ τῶν δικτύων ἐπὶ τὴν ἠόνα, ὡς ἐθεάσατο ἀσπαίροντας, ἔφη· Ὦ κάκιστα ζῷα, ὑμεῖς, ὅτε μὲν ηὔλουν, οὐκ ὠρχεῖσθε· νῦν δέ, ὅτε πέπαυμαι, τοῦτο πράττετε.

43. OF THE FROGGES AND OF JUPYTER

No Thyng is so good as to lyve Justly and at lyberte For fredome and lyberte is better than ony gold or sylver: wherof Esope reherceth to us suche a fable: There were frogges whiche were in dyches and pondes at theyre lyberte: they alle to gyder of one assente & of one wylle maade a request to Jupiter that he wold gyve them a kynge: And Jupiter beganne therof to merveylle: And for theyr kyng he casted to them a grete pyece of wood: whiche maade a grete sowne and noyse in the water: wherof alle the frogges had grete drede and fered moche: And after they approched to theyr kynge for to make obeyssaunce unto hym:

And whanne they perceyved that hit was but a pyece of wood: they torned ageyne to Jupiter prayenge hym swetely that he wold gyve to them another kynge: And Jupiter gaf to them the Heron for to be theyr kynge: And then the Heron beganne to entre in to the water: and ete them one after other: And whanne the frogges sawe that theyr kyng destroyed: and ete them thus: they beganne tendyrly to wepe: sayeng in this manere to the god Jupiter: Ryght hyghe and ryght myghte god Jupiter please the to delyvere us fro the throte of this dragon and fals tyraunt which eteth us the one after another: And he sayd to them: the kynge whiche ye have demounded shalle be your mayster: For whan men have that: which men oughte to have: they ought to be ioyful and glad: And he that hath lyberte ought to kepe hit wel: For nothyng is better than lyberte: For lyberte shold not be wel sold for alle the gold and sylver of all the world.

The Fables of Esope. Translated out of Frensshe in to Englysshe by: William Caxton. With engravings on wood by Agnes Miller Parker. [Wood-engraved initials by William McCance. Compositor: R. Owen Jones.] Newtown, Gregynog Press, 1931. L. 605-1932

The British equivalent of the 'livre d'artiste' was the private press book – just as unattainable for the general public since it usually came out in an expensive limited edition. An outstanding example is the *Gregynog Aesop*, printed in Wales and illustrated by a Scottish artist, Agnes Miller Parker. Through a technique of varied and subtle cutting she has achieved an infinite number of tonal gradations between the extremes of solid black and dazzling white. Light floods in along the diagonal curve of the stream, isolating the frogs clustered together on their rocky promontory.

The Gregynog edition revives Caxton's translation for the first printed English *Aesop* (1483/84), taken from Macho's 1480 French abridgement of Steinhöwel, based on the old French 'Avionnet' (Avianus) and the mediaeval Latin of 'Romulus'. Caxton's woodcuts, redrawn from the Ulm blocks with indifferent skill, play no part in the succession which ends in Barlow, Kirkall and Bewick. Caxton's text, however, was still read as late as the mid-seventeenth century and much paraphrased by other editors. His English is digestible and often delightful; the *promythion* (initial statement) and *epimythion* (moral summing up) have none of the longueurs of a later and more pompous age.

44. THE FOX AND THE SWALLOW

Aristotle informs us that the following fable was spoken by Esop to the Samians, on a debate upon changing their ministers, who were accused of plundering the commonwealth.

A Fox swimming across a river, happened to be entangled in some weeds that grew near the shore, from which he was unable to extricate himself. As he lay thus exposed to whole swarms of flies, who were galling him and sucking his blood; a Swallow observing his distress, kindly offered to drive them away. By no means, said the Fox; for if *these* should be chased away, who are already sufficiently gorged, *another* more hungry swarm would succeed, and I should be robbed of every remaining drop of *blood* in my veins.

Dodsley, 1761

Deliverance from one misfortune can very often lead to something even worse.

Klingspor, 1932

Ein Kalender für das Jahr 1933. Mit Fabeln nach Aesop und Anderen. (Holzstiche von Willi Harwerth.) Offenbach am Main, Gebr. Klingspor [1932]   L. 1684-1935

The early years of this century witnessed a renaissance in the typographical arts, especially in Germany, and productions such as the admirably conceived almanacs (1920-41) from the Klingspor brothers are examples of this new enthusiasm. Klingspor was the first German type-foundry which deliberately set out to employ artists for designing type, evolving a personal 'Klingspor style'. Though not influenced by Morris, Karl Klingspor was an idealist in the same mould.

A different theme and a different treatment were chosen for each calendar; these ranged from astrology to aphorisms or verse. Willi Harwerth was responsible for thirteen of the Klingspor calendars between 1922 and 1939; the calendar of 1922 had brought him to Offenbach where he met Rudolf Koch. Koch, the foremost designer of modern black letter type, lived in Offenbach as a designer and teacher of calligraphy, cooperating intimately with Klingspor. A Koch type was used for Andersen's *The Red Shoes* – published by Douglas Cleverdon in Bristol where Harwerth's woodcuts were hand-coloured, but printed at Offenbach. Delicately tinted woodcuts contrast with the emphatic black-and-white of other twentieth-century *Aesops* (see pp. 119, 133); birds decorate the months and animals the fables. The types are again by Koch: 'Wallau' and 'Magere Wallau'.

Harwerth illustrated mainly the German classics – Goethe and Lessing – and folk tales, working always on a small scale. He is especially known for his volumes done for the Insel-Bücherei in the 1930s and modelled on a predecessor by Koch, but was occupied also with commercial art and the teaching of heraldry.

One of the earliest recorded specimens of Aesop, 'The Fox and the Swallow' is a fable of dictatorship and political corruption (see p. 12). According to Dodsley a hedgehog with ticks had originally been envisaged 'but as that creature seems very unfit for the business of driving away flies, it was thought more proper to substitute the swallow'.

(See colour illustration p. 29)

Der Fuchs und die Schwalbe.

Gar oft kann die Befreiung von einem Übel ein noch är=geres sein.

45. THE CARTER STUCK IN THE MUD

A Haycart stuck fast in a muddy lane.
The luckless Jehu scanned the fields in vain
For human aid. The place was wild and lone,
In darkest Shropshire, near the town of Knighton,
Where, as is generally known,
The Fates plant those they wreak their crowning spite on.
(Pray, reader, lest it be thy lot
To find thyself in such a spot!)
The Charioteer, in his quandary,
Exhausted his vocabulary
Damning with furious oaths and curses
Himself, the road, the cart, the horses.
At last he called upon the name
Of that strong God whose Labours are his fame.
'Help, Hercules!' he cried, 'if once your back
Bore up the firmament and did not crack,
Your arm can get me out of this.'
Straight from the clouds an answer came:
'The Hero likes not laziness.
If you want Hercules to aid you,
Seek first the stumbling-block which has delayed you.
Fill up yon rut: remove this mire and marl
Which to the axle clog your wheels;
Then take your pick to that obstructive stone:
Next beat all level with your heels . . .
Is everything I bade you done?'
'It is,' replied th'obedient carl.
'Then I can help you. Now pick up your whip.'
'I have it. Ha! the wheels have got their grip,
The cart moves on – 'tis magical!
To Hercules the praise be given!'
'See,' said the Voice, ''twas easy after all.
Who helps himself, gets help from Heaven.'

The Fables of Jean de La Fontaine. Translated into English verse by Edward Marsh. With twelve reproductions from engravings by Stephen Gooden. London, William Heinemann, 1933. L. 2476-1933

Stephen Gooden engraved entirely from his own designs, but with an anachronistic attitude characteristically English. A Bible for the Nonesuch Press preceded his *La Fontaine*, and the excellence of his animal engravings led to the commissioning of an *Aesop* in 1936. Adopting Dürer's technique and with the same meticulous craftsmanship, he occasionally creates spatial effects reminiscent of Hollar and other seventeenth-century engravers.

Gooden reintroduced too the engraved architectural title page; his 1931 *La Fontaine* has two title pages (omitted from this cheap edition, as are fourteen plates and the tailpiece vignettes), each framed with the proscenium arch of a puppet theatre. The first volume shows La Fontaine clasping puppets in his arms, replaced for volume II by fable-actors – the Lion and Shepherd. Curiously, the *Esbatement moral* (pp. 46–7) has a similar motif: fable-animals on a stage, the lion at the centre and in the foreground the heads of an unruly pit audience.

This racy adaptation by Sir Edward Marsh, 'a Bohemian in a clean collar' (Beverley Nichols: *Are They the Same at Home?* 1927), usually aims at an archaic idiom but is studded with topical allusions – the 'Shropshire Lad' is one. Sometimes text and illustration appear incompatible partners.

46. THE DONKEY LADEN WITH SPONGES
AND THE DONKEY LADEN WITH SALT

A donkey-driver, sceptre in hand like a Roman emperor, was leading two long-eared steeds. One, laden with sponges, went like an express-runner; the other crept along, needing some coaxing and blows: his load was salt. Our gallant pilgrims travelled up hill and down dale along the donkey-tracks till at last they came to the ford of a river – and a great obstacle they found it. The driver, who was used to crossing that ford every day, mounted the donkey with the sponges, driving the other beast in front – but that donkey wanted his own way and went plunging on into a hole, floated up again and then made his escape, for after a few strokes all his salt had dissolved so completely that his shoulders were freed from the weight. Our friend the sponge-bearer followed his example like a sheep, all in good faith. Now he too was in the water, plunging in up to his neck and taking with him both driver and sponges. Each swallowed as much as the others, the driver and ass as much as the sponges! They immediately became so heavy and filled with so much water that the donkey began to sink and was unable to reach the bank. The driver held on tightly, expecting a speedy and certain death. Someone came to the rescue – it doesn't matter who. It's enough for you to understand from this fable that you should not necessarily imitate your neighbour. That's the point I wished to make.

A.S.H.

La Fontaine: Fables. Eaux-fortes originales de Marc Chagall. Paris, Tériade, 1952.
L. 161-1984

The art dealer and publisher Vollard considered that no illustrator of La Fontaine had yet fully comprehended his complexity: each artist had explored the fables from one angle only, blinkered by his own idiosyncracies or the preoccupations of his period. Believing that Chagall's interpretation might be less literal and more expressive, Vollard asked him to make the attempt, pointing out to hostile French opinion that an Eastern artist would certainly be familiar with La Fontaine's Oriental sources. Chagall's first essays (1926-27) were gouaches, but their intense colour values could not be satisfactorily matched, and so he embarked on one hundred black-and-white drypoint etchings – smaller, and stylistically more uniform. These were printed by Maurice Potin under Vollard's direction (1927-30) but published only after his death, by Tériade. The idiom remained remarkably constant over twenty-five years; for the 1952 covers two further plates were etched by Raymond Haasen.

Over half the designs belong to the early books – the classical Aesopic fables, which Chagall condenses into the 'instant dominant'. Text and illustration do not closely correspond, and the milieu is unspecified, Chagall deliberately distilling the essence of the fable (Bachelard 1952). All areas of the composition seem to be in flux: clouds, sky and weather, constantly in motion, echo the action as if in deference to the Pathetic Fallacy (nature reacts in sympathy with human emotions). Time and space and individual events have become the stuff of legend, and even cruel episodes take on an air of ritual. This freedom of approach combined with the coherence of his conception makes Chagall's re-creation of La Fontaine, from the aesthetic point of view, perhaps the most successful of all twentieth-century interpretations.

47. THE BEE-KEEPER ROBBED AND STUNG

A bee-keeper went visiting in the autumn, and upon his return found that a thief or thieves had carried away all the honeycomb. The provoked, impoverished bees swarmed around him. 'Fools, fools!' he shouted, as he beat them off. 'You look the other way while some stranger helps himself to your winter provisions. Then you sting your old friend who is prepared to feed you sugar until next spring. I've half a mind to go out of business.'

Twelve Fables of Aesop newly narrated by Glenway Wescott and published by the Museum of Modern Art, New York. (Linoleum blocks by Antonio Frasconi.) [Limited edition.] New York, Museum of Modern Art (designed and printed by Joseph Blumenthal at The Spiral Press), 1954. L. 659-1955

Frasconi, an Uruguyan of Italian birth who moved to New York in 1945, has been described as an artist 'capable of being of his time without being either insignificantly abstract or obviously representational' (Una Johnson 1950–51). Starting out as a painter, he became one of the most productive and influential artists of North America and a leader of the woodcut revival, as well as the best-known American fable-illustrator.

Frasconi printed all his cuts himself, using the grain of the wood to achieve rich and varied textures. A first-hand knowledge of late mediaeval woodcuts and block books is reflected in the power and breadth of his designs for children's books and scenes of everyday life. The red-printed titles and heavy black of these linoleum cuts hark back to the dramatic vigour of fifteenth-century Aesops.

The Bee-keeper Robbed and Stung

A bee-keeper went visiting in the autumn, and upon his return found that a thief or thieves had carried away all the honeycomb. The provoked, impoverished bees swarmed around him. "Fools, fools!" he shouted, as he beat them off. "You look the other way while some stranger helps himself to your winter provisions. Then you sting your old friend who is prepared to feed you sugar until next spring. I've half a mind to go out of business."

48. THE HERON

One day the long-necked Heron with his spindle-shanks and long beak was wandering about – I don't know exactly where, but he was following the bank of a river. The stream was as clear as on the finest days; old mother carp was gambolling in a thousand twists and turns with her neighbour the pike. The Heron could easily have taken advantage of them: they were coming near the bank and he had only to seize them. But he thought it better to wait till he had a little more appetite. He was keeping to a diet and ate at fixed times. Quite soon his appetite returned: approaching the bank, he saw some tench emerging from their dwellings deep in the water. A dish such as this did not appeal to him – he was waiting for better things and like Horace's disdainful rat exhibited an exacting palate. 'What, me! eating tench!' he said. 'Why should I, a heron, stoop to such a miserable meal! And who do you take me for?' Having spurned the tench, he next found a gudgeon. 'Gudgeon: that's a fine dinner for a heron! I should open my beak for *that*? God forbid!' He opened it for far less, since it turned out that he saw no more fish at all. Hunger overcame him, and he was only too happy and thankful to encounter a snail.

We ought not to be so particular: the soonest pleased are the wisest. We risk losing all by trying for too much. Be sure to despise nothing, especially when you have found almost *what you want. Many are taken in like this, and it's not to herons that I'm speaking.*

A.S.H.

Jean de La Fontaine: XXIV fables. Burins et bois d'Abram Krol. Paris (Krol), 1959. Presented by the artist L. 1663-1966

In this bibliographical rarity by the *peintre-graveur* Abram Krol, which appeared in an edition of just ninety-nine copies, wood-engraved vignettes accompany the plates as decorative commentary.

Krol develops here the technique of his *Bestiaire*: cut-out copper engravings superimposed on flat two-colour wood engravings – by André Moret – with occasional touches of aquatint (Strahan 1969). Textures are rendered not so much by contours as in a variety of geometric figures, giving an effect two-dimensional and sometimes transparent but with a certain depth. The sandy colours evoke the desert landscapes of several fables – Krol, born in Poland, was for a time in the Foreign Legion. The animals stand severely isolated in the foreground; they are abstractions or timeless symbols, expressing no emotion. A single moment of the action is depicted and all sense of conflict is avoided.

(See colour illustration p. 32)

XVI

49. THE KITE, HAWK, AND PIGEONS

The *Pigeons* finding themselves Persecuted by the *Kite*, made Choice of the *Hawk* for their *Guardian*. The *Hawk* sets up for their Protector; but under Countenance of that Authority, makes more Havock in the *Dove-House* in two Days, than the *Kite* could have done in twice as many Months.

THE MORAL
'Tis a Dangerous Thing for People to call in a Powerful and Ambitious Man for their Protector: And upon the Clamour of here and there a Private Person, to hazard the Whole Community.

REFLECTION

It is highly Dangerous and Imprudent, for a People in War to call in an Enemy Prince to their Defence. There's no Trusting a Perfidious Man, nor any Enmity like the pretended Protection of a Treacherous Friend.

There is no Living in this World without Inconveniencies, and therefore People should have the Wit, or the Honesty, to take up with the Least, and to bear the Lot, which is not to be Avoided, with Honour, and Patience. How many Experiments have been made in the Memory of Man, both in Religion, and in State, to mend Matters, upon pretence that they were Uneasy, *by making them* Intolerable; *And whence is This, but from a Mistaken Opinion of the Present, and as False a Judgment of the Future! And all for want of rightly Understanding the Nature and the Condition of Things, and for want of Foresight into Events. But we are Mad upon Variety, and so Sick of the Present, (how much soever Without, or Against Reason) that we Abandon the Wisdom, and the Providence of Heaven, and Fly from the Grievances of God's Appointment, to Blind Chance for a Remedy. This Fable, in One Word, was never more exactly Moralized, than in our Broils of Famous Memory.*

The Kite was the Evil Counsellor; *The* Free-born People *that complain'd of them were* Pigeons; *The* Hawk *was the Power or Authority that they Appeal'd to for Protection. And what did all this come to at last? The very* Guardians *that took upon them to Rescue the* Pigeons *from the* Kite, *destroy'd the whole* Dove-House, *devour'd the Birds, and shar'd the Spoil amongst Themselves.*

L'Estrange, 6 edn, 1714

Fables of Aesop according to Sir Roger L'Estrange. With fifty drawings by Alexander Calder. New York, Dover Publications, 1967. L. 1932-1976

This reproduction of a scarce limited edition, published with photoetchings in 1931 by Harrison of Paris and also in New York by Minton, Balch & Co made Calder's designs widely available at paperback price. He illustrated La Fontaine in 1948, and an assortment of books with animal subjects.

Calder's creatures might be sculpted in wire, and with their finely-drawn transparent line seem as airborne as his mobiles – yet they are firmly tethered to the page, often being conceived as headpieces or borders to the text. It is hardly surprising that discriminating fable-editors have revived L'Estrange's translation. The first English *Aesop* intended for children, it was caustic and politically aware with a vitality which still leaps from the page.

THE KITE, HAWK, AND PIGEONS

THE pigeons finding themselves perse- cuted by the kite, made choice of the hawk for their guardian. The hawk sets up for their protector; but under countenance of that authority, makes more havock in the dove-house in two days, than the kite could have done in twice as many months.

THE MORAL

'Tis a dangerous thing for people to call in a powerful and an ambitious man for their protector; and upon the clamour of here and there a private person, to hazard the whole community.

63

50. A FOX AND GRAPES

,rish Fox stood gaping under a vine, and licking his lips at a delicious
of grapes he had spied out there; he fetched a hundred leaps at it, till at
ien he found there was no good to be done: Hang 'em, says he, they are as
; crabs; and so away he went.

Samuel Richardson, 1740 [1739]

Those who deceive themselves will be mocked, like the fox in this fable.

Zobel and Hoffmann, 1967

Drei Dutzend Fabeln von Äsop mit ebensoviel Holzschnitten von Felix Hoffmann. [Selected
and adapted from Steinhöwel's *Erneuerter Esopus* or *Ulm Aesop*, 1476/77, by V. Zobel and
F. Hoffmann.] [Zurich, Flamberg-Verlag; Bern] (Angelus Druck, printed by Offizin Winter-
thur AG) [1968]. L.2459-1968

Hoffmann, a Swiss master of the woodcut noted for his fine editions and fairy tale
books, distinguished himself equally in other media, making another set of Aesop
illustrations in coloured glass for the Rathaus in Zofingen. Hoffmann believed in
illustration as an intermediary between author and reader. His fable designs communicate the inherent tension; his austere angular line and use of strong black-
and-white contrast recall earlier styles. As if to drive home this impression the text
is taken from a fifteenth-century translation (see too the *Gregynog Aesop*, p. 118).

The fable of the Fox and the Grapes, with its comprehensive imagery, is an apt
choice for the beginning and ending of this anthology. Traditionally the fox stands
for cunning, hypocrisy and the Devil, and the grape-vine symbolises human sacri-
fice, fertility and wisdom.

Virtues and Vices
A Thematic Analysis in Epithet and Proverb

Now this is but according to the natural Biass of Human Frailty, for every Man to be Partial to his own *Blind-side*, and to Exclaim against the very Counter-part of his Own Daily Practice.

L'Estrange: Preface, 1692

Fable-writers of a religious or didactic persuasion commonly listed their fables by moral as well as by title, categorising them by axiom *and* by actor. Vincent de Beauvais grouped his twenty-nine fables according to vice, and the index to Steinhöwel's *Ulm Aesop* may have been intended as a preacher's aid. Hoogstraten, Draper and Croxall each provided moral indexing, and Dodsley interlarded his fable-contents with explanations.

Fabulists often make general statements on fable. La Fontaine concludes that one must always think things through; La Motte goes even further, declaring 'How imprudent we are, behaving always as if we weren't to die'. Theoreticians of fable catch the habit: to one 'we see ourselves as always guilty' (Blount) and to another we are all 'prisonniers qui de son appétit, qui de son aveuglement' – the resounding rhetoric of Riese-Hubert.

Fables are not so easily explained. All but the simplest are surprisingly ambiguous, allowing considerable flexibility of interpretation – wisely, one mediaeval fabulist, 'Der Stricker', included a second and even a third moral in his index. 'Fraud is call'd wit in one case, good husbandry in another' (L'Estrange: 'Jupiter and Fraud'). Good husbandry may verge on miserliness ('The Ant and the Grasshopper'). The Fox hankering after grapes can be ridiculed or vindicated: to Aphra Behn he symbolised a would-be debaucher of virtue disappointed, but Caxton considered him rather wise. An exhortatory fable used by preachers spells out the moral more clearly ('The Man in the Well', p. 40). Often a subtler message lies hidden beneath the obvious, workaday one, so that the fable must be interpreted on different levels. The underlying moral of 'The Wolf in Sheep's Clothing' is that hypocrisy always overacts and so betrays itself (Dodsley). Again in Dodsley's view, 'The Oak and the Reed' not only tells us to bow before the storm, but that honour and courage are better than mere cleverness or artifice. Fables such as 'The Stag at the Pool' and 'The Dog and Shadow' – the latter incidentally absent from literary fables of the eighteenth century – can be regarded as parables in which the temporal and eternal are opposed.

These fifty fables have been chosen on the basis of their illustrations; viewed thematically the selection takes on a somewhat random air. Some memorable stories have been sacrificed: 'Wolf! Wolf!' for instance, and 'Never count your chickens till they are hatched'. No goose lays golden eggs, nor does the mountain with much ado bring forth a *ridiculus mus*. Lesser-known fables are brought to light and indexed (inevitably with over-simplification) together with more familiar tales – mainly in compared or contrasted pairs or trios of epithets or in proverbs, found convenient by fabulists throughout the centuries.

Analysis by Theme

The principal themes of each fable are indicated in **bold** type.

Adaptability or inflexibility, 34, 94, **110**, 128, 132
Ambition or aspiration, 34, 38-9, 48, 50, 58, 62, 68, 76, 102, 132
Aping one's betters, 58, **62**, **68**, 102
Aping one's neighbours, **124**
Appearances can be misleading, **56**, 64, **66**, 68, 76, 78, 82, 86, 110

Best is enemy of the good, the, 50, 56, 94, **128**
Bird in the hand is worth two in the bush, a, 56, **128**
Biter bit, the, 60, 72, 78, 84, 112

Consistency or inconsistency, 42, 58, **66**, 72, 126
Contentment or dissatisfaction with one's lot, 34, 42, **48**, 50, 56, 76, **94**, 96, 100, **118**, **128**, 130, 132
Contentment or dissatisfaction with one's station in life, 38-9, **48**, 62, 68, 90, 102
Cooperation and peaceful coexistence, 38-9, 70
Courage or cowardice, 46, 104, 110
Courtesy or churlishness, 46, 52, 60, 66, 92, **98**, 108, 126
Crime or punishment, 38-9, 40, 44, 56, 60, 62, 68, 70, 74, 78, 84, 92, 96, 102, 112, 118, 128
Cruelty and mercilessness, 84, 92, 98, 108
Cunning and trickery, 36, 52, **66**, 108; punished, 60, **72**, **78**; rewarded, **54**, **72**, 104, **112**, **114**, 124
Custom and use, 50, **82**, **90**, **100**

Danger or safety, 36, 40, 50, 66, 88, 96, 100, 130
Death, the leveller, 38-9, 40, 48, **80**, 84; fear of, 40-1, 42
Devil you know, the ... , **42**, 48, 50, 100, 118, **120**, 130
Dignity or loss of face, 34, 42, 48, 60, 72, 76, 80, 82, **84**, 86, 102, 110, 114, 128, 132
Disappointment or adversity, 34, 40, 42, 44, 48, 50, 56, 92, 94, 106, 120, 132
Discrimination or lack of judgement, 56, 64, 80, 102, 106, 126, 130

Efforts, all in vain, 40, 44, 54, 56, 62, 68, 116
Endurance and fortitude, 48, **54**, 110, 120
Enemies and oppressors, 36, 66, **84**, 104, 108, 118, 120, **130**
Envy and jealousy, 38-9, 48, 62, 76, 94, 98, 102
Equals, associate with your, 68, **88**, 100

Example is the best precept, **58**, 60; example is not the best precept, 60, 102, **124**

Familiarity breeds contempt, 50, **82**, 96
Fear of the unknown, 42, 66, 82, 88, 100, 120
Flatterers, spongers or impostors, **64**, 70, 78, **114**
Fortune, vicissitudes of, 38-9, **44**, **48**, 50, 54, 56, 68, 84, 92, 110
Fortune-hunters and speculators, 44, **50**, 56
Friends and allies, 36, 52, 66, **88**, 96, **104**, 130

Gentleness or aggression, 36, **54**, 110
Good nature, abused, 36, 52, 60, 64, **82**, **108**, **126**
Gratitude or ingratitude, 36, 46, 52, 60, 66, 94, 96, **108**, **126**
Greed and avarice, 34, 44, **56**, **74**, 98, 132

Honesty, integrity and virtue, 64, 68, 80, 110
Hope and expectation, 34, 44, 50, 56, 74, 118, 128, 130, 132
Humble, insignificant or harmless, the, **46**, 64, 84, 86, 90, 96, 110
Humility and modesty, **38-9**, 68, **90**, 100, 106
Hypocrisy, humbug or bluff, **34**, 52, 60, 62, 66, 68, 72, **78**, 108, 114, **132**

Ignorance, credulity or folly, 36, 40, 50, **52**, 58, 66, 68, 74, 82, 102, **106**, 108, 114, 116, **118**, 124, 126, 130
Improvidence or fecklessness, 86, **92**
Imprudence and rashness, 36, 44, 50, **52**, 62, 74, 86, 88, 102, 108, 112, 118, 124, 130
Impudence and insolence, 38-9, 60, 68, 70, 82, 126
Indolence and sloth, **70**, 86, 92, 122
Industry and application, 70, **86**, **92**
Inner worth, 68, 76, 86
Instinct, will out, 36, **38-9**, **58**; obey the dictates of, 66, 88, 90, 100, 112; beware the dictates of, **74**, 92

Kindness and mercy, **46**

Liberty, value of, 90, 100, **118**
Life, value of, **42**; transience of, 40
Litigation, perils of, 38-9
Luxury, frivolity, ostentation or excess, 40, 58, 62, 68, 70, 86, 92, 100

Majorities and minorities, 108, 130
Maliciousness, *Schadenfreude* and spite, 60, **84**, 92, 98
Man, his own worst enemy, 40, **44**, 50, 56, 74, 94, 118, 128 *and passim*
Man, superiority of, **80**
Meanness and miserliness, 60, 76, 92, 98

Mockery or exposure to ridicule, 34, 38-9, 52, 58, 60, 62, 68, 76, 82, 102, 132

Obstinacy, obsession or self-will, 40, **44**, 50, 118, 124, 128
One man's meat is another man's poison, 60, 80, 88, 94, **100**, 106

Passions, governing one's, 34, 40, 44, 56, 74, 132
Patience, perseverance and resolve, 46, 54, **86**, 122
Peace and tranquillity, 100
Perfidiousness or double-dealing, 36, 52, 60, 66, 72, 78, 104, 108, 126, 130
Perversity and contrariness, 40, 42, 44, 50, 94, 98, 116, 126
Pleasure, transience of, 40, 48, 56, 74, **92**
Political power or corruption, 84, 118, **120**, 130
Powerful and mighty, the, 36, 38-9, 46, 82, 84, 88, 110, 118, **130**
Pride, vanity or affectation, 38-9, 48, **58**, **62**, 68, 76, 80, 84, 86, 96, 102, 110, 114, 128
Prudence, foresight and caution, 36, **52**, 66, 72, 74, 88, 92, 100, 120, 124, 130

Resignation and acceptance, 34, 42, 48, 84, 120, 128, **130**, **132**
Restlessness or longing for variety, 50, 100, 118, 120, 130
Revenge, 68, 74, 78, **84**
Rivalry, competitiveness and strife, 38-9, 54, 62, 86
Rolling stone gathers no moss, a, 50, 88

Season, everything in its, 52, 92, **106**, **116**, 126
Self-deception or self-knowledge and self-criticism, 38-9, 40, 54, 58, 62, 68, 76, 86, 96
Self-indulgence or selfishness, 40, 60, 70, 92, 98
Self-reliance or self-preservation, 42, 52, 64, 66, 72, 92, 104, 110, 122, 124
Self-satisfaction and complacency, 38-9, 48, 58, 68, 70, 86, 92, 110
Soul, the immortal, 40, 80
Spiritual or temporal, the, 40, 56, 76, 96, 106
Stick to your last, 50, **112**, **116**
Strength or weakness, 36, **46**, **54**, 84, 88, 108, **110**, 112
Suffering, universality of, 40

Use before ornament, 68, **90**, 92, **96**, 106

Wit or wisdom, **34**, **38-9**, 40, 52, 54, 106, 120, 128, 130, **132**
Work of all for weal of all, **70**

Sources

The chief sources consulted are listed alphabetically by section or by caption. Direct quotations or detailed references are attributed in full in the text. Sources not included in the Bibliography are cross-referenced, or more fully described.

Five Hundred Years of Illustration and Text

Baur 1974, Blount 1974, Darton 1982, De la Mare 1939, Dodsley 1761, Handford 1973, Hodnett 1976[1], La Motte (Houdart de) 1719, Jacobs 1895, Klingender 1971, Kubičkova [1960?], Küster 1970, Lessing 1982, Quinnam 1966, Reeves 1961, Schiller 1983, Thwaite 1972, Tolkien 1964, Townsend 1882, Varty 1967

History of the Texts

Baur 1974, Blount 1974, Briggs 1971, Bussey 1842, Croxall 1722 (see p.16), Darton 1982, Doderer 1970, 1971, Dodsley 1761, Dyhrenfurth-Gräbsch 1967, Eames 1961, Génot 1980, Goldschmidt 1947, Gottlieb G. 1975, Gottlieb R. 1983, Grant 1958, Hale 1972, Hammelmann 1975, Handford 1973, Hodnett 1976[1], 1979, Jacobs 1889 etc, Klingender 1971, Küster 1969, 1970, L'Estrange 1692 (see p. 16), McKendry 1964, Praz 1964, Quinnam 1966, Richardson 1740 (see p. 16), Schiller 1983, Thwaite 1972, Tiemann H. 1965, TLS 1973, Topsfield 1982, Wilkinson 1929, Wolfenbüttel 1983

Fables and Children

Blount 1974, Darton 1982, Doderer 1970, 1971, Dyhrenfurth-Gräbsch 1967, Génot 1980, Gottlieb G. 1975, Gottlieb R. 1983, Hale 1972, Handford 1973, Hobbs M. 1983 (talk: The English Aesop Illustrated), Hodnett 1976[1], Jacobs 1894 etc, Küster 1970, La Fontaine 1668, Landwehr 1963, L'Estrange 1692 (see p. 16), Osborne 1966 etc, Quinnam 1966, Thwaite 1972

History of the Illustrations

Baltimore 1984, Baur 1974, Bland 1969, Blount 1974, Darton 1982, Doderer 1970, 1971, Erber 1980/81, Génot 1980, Goldschmidt 1947, Hale 1972, Harms 1980, Harrop 1980, Hearn 1977, Hobbs M. 1983 (see above), Hodnett 1971, 1973, 1976[1], 1976[2], 1979, Holloway 1969, Klingender 1971, Küster 1969, 1970, McKendry 1964, Martin 1982-, Opperman 1977, Riese-Hubert 1967, Scheler 1966, Tiemann H. 1965, TLS 1973, Wolfenbüttel 1983

Fables and Society

Blount 1974, Darton 1982, Doderer 1970, Hale 1972, Hodnett 1976[1], Jacobs 1895, Klingender 1971, Küster 1969, 1970, Reeves 1961, Varty 1967, Wolfenbüttel 1983

Captions (major sources only)

endpapers Bland 1969, Gottlieb G. 1975
page 3 Hobbs M. 1983 (see above), Küster 1970, Wolfenbüttel 1983
page 10 Wolfenbüttel 1983

1. Hodnett 1976[1], 1979, Küster 1970, Wolfenbüttel 1983
2. Donati 1948, Geldner 1970, Häbler 1924, Hodnett 1976[1], Klingender 1971, Küster 1970, Lippmann 1888, Stern 1970, TLS 1973
3. Bland 1969, Hodnett 1971, Küster 1970, Landwehr 1963, Wolfenbüttel 1983
4. Bary 1958, Quinnam 1966, Topsfield 1982, Wolfenbüttel 1983
5. Gottlieb G. 1975, Hodnett 1979, Johnson A.F. 1928, Küster 1969, Tiemann H. 1965
6. Hale 1972, Hodnett 1979, Küster 1970, Mandowsky 1961, Praz 1964
7. Hodnett 1971, 1979, Küster 1969, Scheler 1966, Tiemann H. 1965, Wolfenbüttel 1983
8. Hodnett 1971, 1979, Küster 1969, Scheler 1966, Tiemann H. 1965
9. Hobbs M. 1983 (see above), Küster 1970, Wolfenbüttel 1983
10. Hodnett 1979, Küster 1970
11. Hale 1972, Hodnett 1979, Quinnam 1966
12. Hale 1972, Hodnett 1979, Wolfenbüttel 1983
13. Hodnett 1979, McKendry 1964
14. Bland 1969, Quinnam 1966, Wolfenbüttel 1983
15. Gottlieb G. 1975, Hodnett 1979
16. Bland 1969, Hodnett 1971, 1979, Küster 1969, Scheler 1966, Tiemann H. 1965
17. Hodnett 1979, Scheler 1966, Wolfenbüttel 1983
18. Hodnett 1971, Tiemann H. 1965
19. Bussey 1842, Hammelmann 1975, Wolfenbüttel 1983
20. Baltimore 1984, Bland 1969, Génot 1980, McKendry 1964, Martin 1982-, Opperman 1977, Quinnam 1966, Riese-Hubert 1967
21. Baltimore 1984, Bland 1969
22. Hammelmann 1952, Quinnam 1966
23. Hodnett 1979, Quinnam 1966, Wolfenbüttel 1983
24. Hobbs M. 1983 (see above), Keynes 1972
25. Baur 1974
26. Bussey 1842, Hodnett 1976[2], 1979, Johnson G.C. 1983, Thwaite 1972
27. Bland 1969, Hodnett 1979, Osborne 1966 etc, Quinnam 1966
28. Doderer 1971, Quinnam 1966, Riese-Hubert 1967
29. Doderer 1971, Dyhrenfurth-Gräbsch 1967, Wolfenbüttel 1983
30. Génot 1980, Riese-Hubert 1967
31. Bland 1969, McKendry 1964
32. Townsend 1882, Wolfenbüttel 1983
33. Bland 1969, Blount 1974, Gottlieb G. 1975
34. Bland 1969, McKendry 1964, Quinnam 1966, Riese-Hubert 1967, Wolfenbüttel 1983
35. Bland 1969, Blount 1974, Osborne 1966 etc, Quinnam 1966
36. Blount 1974, Hobbs M. 1983 (see above)
37. Hearn 1977, Osborne 1966 etc, Quinnam 1966, Wolfenbüttel 1983
38. Blount 1974, Darton 1982, Engen 1975, Hearn 1977, McKendry 1964, Spencer 1975
39. Blount 1974
40. Gettings 1975, Hudson 1960
41. Bénézit 1976, Kahn 1919-20, Wolfenbüttel 1983
42. Blamires 1971, Cleverdon 1983, Fleuron VI 1928, Lucie-Smith 1981, National Book League 1972, Tate Gallery 1981, Victoria and Albert Museum 1985
43. Harrop 1980, Hodnett 1976[1]
44. Cleverdon 1983, Dodsley 1761, Rodenberg 1926, Schauer 1963, Semrau 1975, Windisch 1928 (Fleuron VI)
45. Bland 1969, Dodgson 1944, Keynes 1981, Lewis 1967 (The Twentieth Century Book), Quinnam 1966, Reid 1932
46. Derrière le Miroir 1952, Riese-Hubert 1967, Strahan 1969, Tate Gallery 1985, Victoria and Albert Museum 1985, Wolfenbüttel 1983
47. Erber 1981, Johnson U.E. 1950-51, Quinnam 1966
48. Doderer 1971, Riese-Hubert 1967, Strahan 1969, Wolfenbüttel 1983
49. Erber 1981, Quinnam 1966
50. Erber 1981, Wendland 1967, Wolfenbüttel 1983

Virtues and Vices

Blount 1974, Darton 1982, Doderer 1970, Dodsley 1761, Gottlieb R. 1983, La Motte (Houdart de) 1719, McKendry 1964, Riese-Hubert 1967

Bibliography

IA GENERAL WORKS ON BIBLIOGRAPHY AND THE HISTORY OF PRINTING

British Library General Catalogue of Printed Books to 1975 London, 1980

Brunet, Jacques Charles *Manuel du libraire et de l'amateur de livres* (5 edn) Paris, Firmin-Didot, 1860-65 (*Supplément*) 1878-80

Cambridge Bibliography *The New Cambridge Bibliography of English Literature* Cambridge, University Press, 1969-77

Cartier, Alfred *Bibliographie des éditions des de Tournes, imprimeurs lyonnais* Paris, Éditions des Bibliothèques Nationales de France, 1938

Geldner, Ferdinand *Die deutschen Inkunabeldrucker: ein Handbuch der deutschen Buchdrucker des XV. Jahrhunderts nach Druckorten* Stuttgart, Hiersemann, 1970 [and other works by Geldner]

Gesamtkatalog der Wiegendrucke Leipzig, Berlin, Kommission für den Gesamtkatalog, 1925-38

Häbler, Konrad *Die deutschen Buchdrucker des XV. Jahrhunderts im Auslande* Munich, Rosenthal, 1924

Hain, Ludovicus *Repertorium bibliographicum* Stuttgart, J. G. Cotta, 1826-38

Lewine, Jacob *Bibliography of Eighteenth Century Art and Illustrated Books* London, Sampson Low, Marston & Co, 1898

Pollard, Alfred William and Redgrave, Gilbert Richard *A Short-title Catalogue of Books Printed in England ... 1475-1640* London, Bibliographical Society, 1926

Praz, M. *Studies in Seventeenth-century Imagery* See IB

Wing, Donald Godard *Short-title Catalogue of Books Printed in England ... 1641-1700* (2 edn) New York, Modern Language Association of America, Index Committee, 1972-

IB Bibliography of Fables

Barbier, – *Notice des principales éditions des fables et des œuvres de Jean de La Fontaine* In *Fables inédites des XIIe, XIIIe et XIVe siècles et Fables de La Fontaine* Paris, Cubin, 1825

Keidel, George C. *A Manual of Aesopic Fable Literature [up to] 1500* (*Romance and Other Studies* II) Baltimore, Friedenwald Co, 1896

Küster, Christian Ludwig *Illustrierte Aesop-Ausgaben des 15. und 16. Jahrhunderts* (*Dissertation*) Hamburg, University, 1970

Landwehr, John *Dutch Emblem Books: a Bibliography* (*Bibliotheca emblematica*) Utrecht, Haentjens Dekker & Gumbert, 1962

Landwehr, John *Fable-books Printed in the Low Countries: a Concise Bibliography until 1800* Nieuwkoop, De Graaf, 1963

Landwehr, John *Emblem Books in the Low Countries, 1554-1949: a Bibliography* (*Bibliotheca emblematica*) Utrecht, Haentjens Dekker & Gumbert, 1970

Praz, Mario *Studies in Seventeenth-century Imagery* (2 edn) (*Sussidi eruditi* 16) Rome, Edizioni di Storia e Letteratura, 1964

Quinnam, Barbara (compiled by) *Fables from Incunabula to Modern Picture Books: a Selective Bibliography* Washington, Library of Congress, General Reference and Bibliography Division, Reference Department, 1966

Schiller, Justin G. *Realms of Childhood* (*Catalogue* 43) New York, 1983

IC Fables in Children's Literature

Blount, M. *Animal Land: the Creatures of Children's Fiction* See II

Darton, F. J. Harvey *Children's Books in Britain: Five Centuries of Social Life* (3 edn revised by Brian Alderson) Cambridge, University Press, 1982

Dyhrenfurth-Gräbsch, Irene *Geschichte des deutschen Jugendbuchs* (3 edn) Zurich, Atlantis, 1967

Gottlieb, Gerald (captions to) *Early Children's Books and their Illustrators* [in the Pierpont Morgan Library, New York] London, Oxford University Press, 1975

Gottlieb, Robin *Jean de La Fontaine and Children* In *Hornbook Magazine* LIX, p. 25, Feb 1983

The Osborne Collection of Early Children's Books, 1566-1910 (vol II 1476-1910) (2 edn compiled by Judith St. John and others) Toronto, Public Library, 1966, 1975

Schiller, J. G. *Realms of Childhood* See IB

Thwaite, Mary F. *From Primer to Pleasure in Reading* (2 edn) London, Library Association of Great Britain, 1972

II HISTORY AND THEORY OF FABLES

Bary, William Theodore de (edited by) *Sources of Indian Tradition* I (*Introduction to Oriental Civilizations*) New York and London, Columbia University Press, 1958

Blount, Margaret *Animal Land: the Creatures of Children's Fiction* London, Hutchinson, 1974

Briggs, Katharine M. *Fables and Exempla* In *A Dictionary of British Folk-tales in the English Language* A, II: *Folk Narratives* 1 London, Routledge & Kegan Paul, 1971

Bussey, G. Moir *Introductory Dissertation on the History of Fable* In *Fables, Original and Selected* London, Willoughby & Co, 1842

Costello, Louisa Stuart *The Rose Garden of Persia* London, Longman, Brown, Green, Longmans, 1845

De la Mare, Walter (introduction to his) *Animal Stories* London, Faber, 1939

Doderer, Klaus *Fabeln: Formen, Figuren, Lehren* Zurich, Atlantis, 1970

Dodsley, Robert *An Essay on Fable* In his *Select Fables of Esop and Other Fabulists* Birmingham, by John Baskerville for R. & J. Dodsley, 1761

Gottlieb, G. *Early Children's Books and their Illustrators* See IC

Gottlieb, R. *Jean de La Fontaine and Children* See IC

Grant, Michael *Roman Literature* (rev edn) Harmondsworth, Penguin, 1958

Green, Rev Henry *Andrea Alciati and his Books of Emblems* London, Trübner, 1872

Hale, David G. *Aesop in Renaissance England* In *The Library* XXVII (5th series), 2, p. 116, June 1972

Handford, S. A. (introduction to) *Fables of Aesop* Harmondsworth, Penguin Classics, 1954 (reprint) 1973

Harms, W. *Daniel Wilhelm Trillers Auffassung von der Fabel* etc. See IIIB

Hodnett, Edward[1] (introduction to) *The History and Fables of Aesop* [facsimile of Caxton's edition] London, Scolar Press, 1976

Houdart de La Motte, Antoine *Discours sur la fable* In his *Fables nouvelles* Paris, by Coignard for Dupuis, 1719

Jacobs, Joseph (introductions to) *The Fables of Aesop as first printed by William Caxton ... now again edited ... by J.J.* London, Nutt, 1889 (*Bibliothèque de Carabas* 4, 5); *The Fables of Aesop Selected* London, New York, Macmillan & Co, 1894

Klingender, Francis Donald *Animals in Art and Thought to the End of the Middle Ages* London, Routledge & Kegan Paul, 1971

La Fontaine, Jean de *Préface* to his

Fables choisies, mises en vers Paris, Denys Thierry, 1668

Landwehr, J. *Fable-books Printed in the Low Countries* See IB

Lessing, Doris (introduction to) *Kalila and Dimna: Selected Fables of Bidpai* retold by Ramsay Wood London, Granada, 1982

Praz, M. *Studies in Seventeenth-century Imagery* See IB

Quinnam, B. *Fables from Incunabula to Modern Picture Books* See IB

Reeves, James (introduction to) *Fables from Aesop* London & Glasgow, Blackie, 1961

Robert, A. C. M. *Notice sur les fabulistes* In *Fables inédites des XIIe, XIIIe et XIVe siècles et* Fables de La Fontaine Paris, Cubin, 1825

Somadeva Bhaṭṭa *The Ocean of Story, being C. H. Tawney's Translation of Somadeva's* Kathā Sarit Sāgara *(or Ocean of Streams of Story)* edited by N. M. Penzer London, privately printed, 1924–28

Stern, Simon (introduction to) *The Life and Fables of Aesop: a Selection from the Version of Sir Roger L'Estrange* London, Kahn & Averill, Stanmore Press, 1970

Thompson, Stith *Motif-index of Folk-literature* (rev edn) Copenhagen, Rosenkilde & Bagger, 1955–58

Tiemann, Barbara *Fabel und Emblem: Gilles Corrozet und die französische Renaissance-Fabel (Humanistische Bibliothek I, 18)* Munich, Fink, 1974

Tiemann, H. *Wort und Bild in der Fabeltradition* See IIIB

Tolkien, J. R. R. *On Fairy-stories* In *Tree and Leaf* London, Allen & Unwin, 1964

Topsfield, Andrew *A Mirror for Princes* In *Times Literary Supplement* 4118, p. 267, 5 Mar 1982

Townsend, Rev George Fyler *Aesop and his Fables* In *Aesop's Fables* London, Routledge, 1882

Wilkinson, J. V. S. *The Lights of Canopus: Anvár i Suhailí* See IIIC (2)

Wolfenbüttel, Herzog August Bibliothek *Fabula docet: illustrierte Fabelbücher aus sechs Jahrhunderten* See IIIB

IIIA GENERAL WORKS ON BOOK ILLUSTRATION

Baltimore, Museum of Art *Regency to Empire: French Printmaking, 1715–1814* [exhibition] 1984

Bénézit, E. *Dictionnaire . . . des peintres, sculpteurs* etc. (new edn) Paris, Gründ, 1976

Bland, David *The History of Book Illustration* (2 edn) London, Faber, 1969

Hodnett, Edward *English Woodcuts, 1480–1535* (rev edn) Oxford, University Press, 1973 *Additions and Corrections*

London, Bibliographical Society (*Illustrated Monograph* XXIIa) 1973

Holloway, Owen E. *French Rococo Book Illustration (Chapters in Art)* London, Tiranti, 1969

Kristeller, Paul *Kupferstich und Holzschnitt in vier Jahrhunderten* (2 edn) Berlin, Cassirer, 1911

Lewine, J. *Bibliography of Eighteenth Century Art and Illustrated Books* See IA

London, Victoria and Albert Museum *From Manet to Hockney: Modern Artists' Illustrated Books* edited by Carol Hogben and Rowan Watson 1985

Martin, Henri Jean *Histoire de l'édition française* Paris, Promodis, 1982–

Reid, Forrest *Illustrators of the Sixties* London, Faber & Gwyer, 1925

Strachan, Walter John *The Artist and the Book in France: the 20th Century 'livre d'artiste'* London, Owen, 1969

Thieme, Ulrich and Becker, Felix *Allgemeines Lexikon der bildenden Künstler von der Antike bis zur Gegenwart* Leipzig, Engelmann (Seemann), 1907–50

IIIB Illustration of Fables: General Studies

Baur, Otto *Bestiarium humanum: Mensch-Tier-Vergleich in Kunst und Karikatur* Munich, Moos, 1974

Blount, M. *Animal Land: the Creatures of Children's Fiction* See II

Dalban, C. and Droz, E. *Étude sur l'illustration des fables* In *Livres à gravures imprimés à Lyon au XVe siècle* IV: *Les subtiles fables d'Esope, Lyon, Mathieu Husz, 1486* Lyons, Association Guillaume Le Roy, 1926

Doderer, K. *Fabeln: Formen, Figuren, Lehren* See II

Doderer, Klaus *Ilustrácia zvieracej bájky v detskej literatúre/Illustration of Fables in the Literature for Children* In *Zborník* IV, i, p. 143 (*Bienále Ilustrácií, Bratislava '71*) Bratislava, Slovenská Národná Galéria, 1976

Erber, Ulrike *Der Fuchs und der Rabe: kleiner Streifzug durch die Fabelillustration* In *Illustration 63* XVII, 3, p. 103, 1980; XVIII, 1, p. 23, 1981

Gottlieb, G. *Early Children's Books and their Illustrators* See IC

Harms, Wolfgang *Daniel Wilhelm Trillers Auffassung von der Fabel im Titelblatt und in Rahmentexten seiner 'Neuen Aesopischen Fabeln' von 1740* In Meier, Christel and Ruberg, Uwe *Text und Bild* Wiesbaden, Reichert, 1980

Hodnett, Edward *Aesop in England: the Transmission of Motifs in Seventeenth-century Illustrations of Aesop's Fables* Charlottesville, University of Virginia Bibliographical Society, 1979

Hodnett, E. See also II, IIIC (1)

Klingender, F. D. *Animals in Art and Thought* See II

Küster, C. L. *Illustrierte Aesop-Ausgaben* See IB

McKendry, John J. (edited by) *Aesop: Five Centuries of Illustrated Fables* New York, Metropolitan Museum of Art; Spiral Press, 1964

Quinnam, B. *Fables from Incunabula to Modern Picture Books* See IB

Scheler, Lucien *La Persistance du motif dans l'illustration flamande des fables d'Esope du seizième au dix-huitième siècle* In *Studia bibliographica in honorem Herman de la Fontaine Verwey*, p. 350 Amsterdam, Hertzberger, 1966 (1968)

Schiller, J. G. *Realms of Childhood* See IB

Stern, S. *The Life and Fables of Aesop* See II

Tiemann, B. *Fabel und Emblem* See II

Tiemann, Hermann *Wort und Bild in der Fabeltradition bis zu La Fontaine* In *Buch und Welt: Festschrift für Gustav Hofmann* Wiesbaden, Harrassowitz, 1965

Wolfenbüttel, Herzog August Bibliothek *Fabula docet: illustrierte Fabelbücher aus sechs Jahrhunderten* [exhibition from the Library and the Kritter collection, with catalogue by U. Bodemann and others] 1983

IIIC (1) Illustration of Fables: Special Studies (*illustrators and printers*)

EARLY BOOKS AND MANUSCRIPTS

Donati, Lamberto *Discorso sulle illustrazioni dell' Esopo di Napoli, 1485, e sulla 'Passio' zilografico* In *Bibliofilia* L, p. 53, 1948

Goldschmidt, Adolph *An Early Manuscript of the Aesop Fables of Avianus and Related Manuscripts (Studies in Manuscript Illumination* I) Princeton, University Press, 1947

Green, Rev H. *Andrea Alciati and his Books of Emblems* See II

Johnson, Alfred Forbes *Geofroy Tory* [including his influence on early *Aesops*] In *Fleuron* VI, p. 37, 1928

Kristeller, Paul (introduction to) *Der Edelstein* [facsimile of 1461 edn] Berlin, Graphische Gesellschaft (*Ausserordentliche Veröffentlichungen* II) 1908 1908

Lippmann, Friedrich *The Art of Wood-engraving in Italy in the Fifteenth Century* [including the *Naples Aesop*] London, Quaritch, 1888

Stern, S. *The Life and Fables of Aesop* [on the *Naples Aesop*] See II

Times Literary Supplement 3744, p. 1515, 7 Dec 1973 *A Renaissance Book Reborn* [on the *Naples Aesop*]

BARLOW

Hodnett, Edward *Francis Barlow: First*

Master of English Book Illustration
London, Scolar Press; Berkeley, University
of California Press, 1978
    Hodnett, E. *Aesop in England* See IIIB
BEWICK
    Hodnett, E. *Aesop in England* See IIIB
BLAKE
    Keynes, Sir G. L. *Blake's Engravings for
Gay's Fables* See IIIC (2)
CALDECOTT
    Hearn, Michael Patrick (introduction
to) *The Caldecott Aesop: 20 Fables Illus-
trated by Randolph Caldecott. A Facsimile*
New York, Doubleday, 1977 (1978)
CHAGALL
    Derrière le Miroir See IIIC (2)
    London, Tate Gallery *Chagall*
[exhibition, by Susan Compton] 1985
CHAUVEAU
    Biard, J. D. *François Chauveau:
vignettes des* Fables de La Fontaine *(1668)*
See IIIC (2)
CLEYN
    Hodnett, E. *Aesop in England* See IIIB
CRANE
    Engen, Rodney K. *Walter Crane as a
Book Illustrator* London, Academy, 1975
    Spencer, Isobel *Walter Crane* London,
Studio Vista, 1975
FRASCONI
    Baltimore, Museum of Art *The Work
of Antonio Frasconi, 1952-1963* 1963
    Cleveland, Museum of Art *The Work
of Antonio Frasconi* 1952
    Johnson, Una E. *The Woodcuts of
Antonio Frasconi* In *Print* VI, 4, p. 33,
1950-51
GHEERAERTS
    Hodnett, Edward *Marcus Gheeraerts
the Elder of Bruges, London and Antwerp*
Utrecht, Haentjens Dekker & Gumbert,
1971
    Hodnett, E. *Francis Barlow: First
Master of English Book Illustration* See
under BARLOW
    Hodnett, E. *Aesop in England* See IIIB
    Küster, Christian Ludwig *Bemerkungen
zum emblematischen Fabelbuch 'De
Warachtighe Fabulen der Dieren' von
1567* In *Raggi: Zeitschrift für
Kunstgeschichte und Archäologie* IX, 4, p.
113, 1969
    Tiemann, H. *Wort und Bild in der
Fabeltradition bis zu La Fontaine* See IIIB
GOODEN
    Dodgson, Campbell *An Iconography of
the Engravings of Stephen Gooden*
London, Elkin Mathews, 1944
    Keynes, Sir Geoffrey Langdon *The
Gates of Memory* Oxford, University
Press, 1981
    Reid, Forrest *The Line Engravings of
Stephen Gooden* In *Print Collector's
Quarterly* XIX, p. 51, 1932

HARWERTH
    Schauer, Georg Kurt *Deutsche
Buchkunst, 1890 bis 1960* Hamburg,
Maximilian-Gesellschaft, 1963
    Semrau, Eberhard *Der Illustrator und
Graphiker Willi Harwerth* In *Illustration 63*
II, 1, p. 8, 1975
HELLÉ
    Kahn, Gustave *André Hellé* In *L'Art et
les Artistes* I (N.S.), p. 337, 1919-20
HOFFMANN
    Wendland, Henning *Felix Hoffmann:
seine Arbeit im Buch, in Glas, auf der
Wand* Aarau & Frankfurt, Sauerländer,
1971
HOLLAR
    Hodnett, E. *Aesop in England* See IIIB
JONES
    Blamires, David *David Jones, Artist
and Writer* Manchester, University Press,
1971
    Cleverdon, Douglas *Stanley Morison
and Eric Gill, 1925-1933* In *Book
Collector* XXXII, i, 1983
    Fleuron VI, pp. xi, 231, 1928 *Seven
Fables of Aesop* [note in Contents, and
type review]
    London, National Book League *David
Jones* [exhibition] 1972
    London, Tate Gallery *David Jones*
[exhibition] 1981
    Lucie-Smith, Edward *David Jones at
the Tate* In *Illustrated London News* 269,
no. 6997, p. 85, Aug 1981
KIRKALL
    Hodnett, Edward[2] *Elisha Kirkall,
c. 1682-1742: Master of White-line
Engraving in Relief and Illustrator of
Croxall's Aesop* In *Book Collector* 25,
ii, p. 195, Summer 1976
    Hodnett, E. *Aesop in England* See IIIB
    Johnson, G. C. *Croxall's Fables of 1722:
the Nature of the Engravings* In *Book
Collector* 32, iii, p. 315, Autumn 1983
KLINGSPOR
    Rodenberg, Julius *The Work of Karl
Klingspor* In *Fleuron* V, p. 1, 1926
LIGORIO
    Mandowsky, Erna *Pirro Ligorio's
Illustrations to Aesop's Fables* In *Journal
of the Warburg and Courtauld Institutes*
XXIV, p. 327, 1961
OUDRY
    Opperman, Hal N. *Jean-Baptiste Oudry*
(Outstanding Dissertations in the Fine Arts)
New York & London, Garland, 1977
PARKER
    Harrop, Dorothy A. *A History of the
Gregynog Press* Pinner, Private Libraries
Association, 1980
RACKHAM
    Gettings, Fred *Arthur Rackham*
London, Studio Vista, 1975
    Hudson, Derek *Arthur Rackham: his

Life and Work London, Heinemann, 1960
TAYLOR
    Hammelmann, Hanns A. *Eighteenth-
century English Illustrators: Isaac Taylor
the Elder* In *Book Collector* 1, i, p. 14,
Spring 1952

IIIC (2) Illustration of Fables: Special
Studies *(collections)*

BĪDPĀĪ
    Costello, L. S. *The Rose Garden of
Persia* See II
    Kubičková, Věra *Persian Miniatures*
London, Spring Books [1960?]
    Quinnam, B. *Fables from Incunabula to
Modern Picture Books* See IB
    Topsfield, A. *A Mirror for Princes* See II
    Verve I, iii, p. 26, 1937 *Bidpai,
Forefather of Fables*
    Wilkinson, James Vere Stuart *The
Lights of Canopus:* Anvár i Suhailí London,
Studio, 1929
GAY
    Hammelmann, Hanns A. *Book
Illustrators in Eighteenth-century England*
(Studies in British Art) London, Paul
Mellon Foundation for British Art, 1975
    Keynes, Sir Geoffrey Langdon *Blake's
Engravings for Gay's Fables* In *Book
Collector* 21, 1, p. 59, Spring 1972
LA FONTAINE
    Biard, J. D. (introduction to) *François
Chauveau: vignettes des* Fables de La
Fontaine *(1668)* (Textes littéraires XXIV)
Exeter, University, 1977
    Derrière le Miroir 44-45, 1952 [special
number on Chagall's *La Fontaine* by
Bachelard, Vollard and others]
    Després, Armand *Les Éditions illustrées
des* Fables de La Fontaine Paris,
Rouquette & Fils, 1892-93
    Génot, Ch. H. *La Cigale et la fourmi:
illustration des* Fables de La Fontaine In
Gazette des Beaux-Arts XCV, p. 71, 1980
    Gottlieb, R. *Jean de La Fontaine and
Children* See IC
    Riese-Hubert, Renée *Interpretation
figurée des* Fables de La Fontaine In Paris,
Comité national de la Gravure française
Nouvelles de L'Estampe 3, p. 92, 1967
OGILBY
    Eames, Marian *John Ogilby and his
Aesop* In *Bulletin of the New York Public
Library* 65, p. 77, 1961
REYNARD THE FOX
    Jacobs, Joseph (introduction to) *The
Most Delectable History of Reynard the
Fox* London, Macmillan & Co, 1895
    Varty, Kenneth *Reynard the Fox: a
Study of the Fox in Medieval English Art*
Leicester, University Press, 1967

Index

25 Love and Folly.	26 The Eclipse.	27 The Boy and ye Butterfly.
28 The Toad & the Ephemeron.	29 The Peacock.	30 The Fly in St Paul's Cupola.
31 The Elm-tree and the Vine.	32 The Laurustinus & the Rose-tree.	33 The Sentivive Plant & Palm-tree.
34 The Sentyrites & ye Ichneumon.	35 The Tulip & the Rose.	36 The Woodcock and Mallard.